Earnings Quality

Elisa Menicucci

Earnings Quality

Definitions, Measures, and Financial Reporting

palgrave
macmillan

Elisa Menicucci
University of Roma Tre
Rome, Italy

ISBN 978-3-030-36797-8 ISBN 978-3-030-36798-5 (eBook)
https://doi.org/10.1007/978-3-030-36798-5

This Palgrave Pivot imprint is published by the registered company Springer Nature Switzerland AG
The registered company address is: Gewerbestrasse 11, 6330 Cham, Switzerland

Preface

In recent years, earnings quality (EQ) has received more and more attention from investors, creditors, regulators, and researchers in different areas. Financial statements are the main source of information for stakeholders, and especially, income represents the most important accounting information that managers, directors, investors, and other stakeholders rely on for their decisions. In this regard, one issue is whether accounting information copes satisfactorily with such a wide variety of information needs.

Since earnings are assumed as the basis for most of decisions, assessment models, and stock pricing, the income statement needs to be of high quality to assure reliability, accuracy, and informativeness of accounting information. However, the amount of earnings cannot be always a good criterion for investors' decision-making since sometimes earnings are manipulated by management. Hence, users of financial reporting have to note both the quantity and the quality of earnings. In this context, researchers have proposed different definitions of EQ since it is a multi-dimensional and broad concept encompassing many determinants. Moreover, there is not a generally accepted approach to measure EQ, although a variety of proxies have been developed in recent years.

The purpose of this book is to provide an overview for understanding EQ in the context of financial reporting and to offer suggestions for defining and measuring it. We also turn our attention to earnings management (EM) and its effect on EQ. EM occurs when managers make discretionary accounting choices that are regarded as either an efficient communication of private information to improve the informativeness of a firm's current and future performance or a distorting disclosure to mislead the true performance of the firm. The intentional manipulation of earnings by managers, within the limits allowed by the Accounting Standards, may alter the usefulness of financial reporting and imply a lower quality of earnings.

The book goes on to elaborate on EQ in the context of International Financial Reporting Standards (IAS/IFRSs) and in particular the question focused on both the degree of EM and the value relevance of reported earnings in such a setting. The use of Fair Value in financial reporting has developed a current debate about the impact of Fair Value Accounting (FVA) on EQ. Sometimes, the high degree of subjectivity in estimating Fair Value could allow opportunities for managers to exercise judgments and intentional bias which can decrease the quality of financial reporting. In this regard, management discretion can result in a higher EM and thus in a reduced amount of EQ. Especially during periods of financial distress, managers engage in EM to mask the negative effects of the turmoil (e.g., low profitability and bad financial performance).

The book is organized as follows. The first chapter offers a brief literature review on the concept of EQ and provides an overview of its possible definitions as accounting literature does not provide an explicit and unique definition of EQ. Despite the importance of earnings within financial reporting, the term EQ is vague and has different interpretations. In Chapter 2, we present the multiplicity of proxies that can be used to measure EQ. We analyze the existing plenty of acceptable methods for EQ measurement that depends on the research question posed and the availability of data and estimation models. Chapter 3 describes the relationship between EQ and EM since they can be considered related challenges in financial reporting. Chapter 4 deepens the issue of IAS/IFRSs and their impact on accounting quality. Given the emphasis on the use of Fair Value and the greater disclosure requirements recommended by IAS/IFRSs, the adoption of these Standards has some effects on the quality of earnings reported by companies. Finally, Chapter 5 discusses the theoretical background of FVA and focuses on the impact it might have on EQ. We investigate how FVA influences earnings manipulation (i.e., EM), value relevance, and informativeness of reported earnings in periods of financial distress as accruals and earnings smoothing are attempts of managers to reduce abnormal variations of earnings, especially during a turmoil.

Rome, Italy Elisa Menicucci

Contents

List of Tables

CHAPTER 1

Earnings Quality: How to Define

Abstract The concept of earnings quality (EQ) is a significant topic attracting considerable attention within the financial reporting process. In literature, there is no an agreed-upon definition for EQ or a generally accepted methodology for measuring it. Different studies focus on one or more aspects of earnings, i.e., the persistence, the informativeness, sustainability, stability, predictability, and lack of variability of reported earnings. Moreover, EQ is contextual as it has different meanings to different financial statements' users. Thus, the term "earnings quality" alone is meaningless as it can be defined only in the context of a specific decision model. First, EQ is conditional on the decision relevance of the information. Second, the quality of earnings depends on whether it is informative about the firm's financial performance.

Keywords Earnings quality (EQ) · Definitions · Usefulness · Informativeness · Financial reporting

1.1 Introduction

Financial statements are one of the key elements of decision-making process in capital markets, and especially, income represents the most important accounting information that investors, managers, directors,

E. Menicucci, *Earnings Quality*,
https://doi.org/10.1007/978-3-030-36798-5_1

and regulators rely on for their decisions. Accuracy, reliability, assurance, predictability, timeliness, and realization of income have a direct relationship mainly with investment appraisals. Therefore, the income statement needs to be of high quality to insure reliability, accuracy, and informativeness of accounting information since the bottom line of the income statement is assumed as the basis for most of decisions, assessment models, and stock pricing.

There is a large amount of literature investigating the impact of companies' information on analysts' forecasts. The information environment of a company is considered a key driver of forecasts' accuracy, as the quantity and the quality of the available information may reduce uncertainty about future prospects and thus may contribute to reduce forecast errors. One of the main attributes of the information setting of an entity is the extent of financial disclosure, and in this regard, several papers have shown that financial reporting is an important source of information used by financial analysts for predictive purposes (e.g., Aktas & Kargin, 2012; Armstrong, Gyay, & Weber, 2010; Peek, 2005). However, it is not yet clear whether it is the quantity or the quality of financial information that drives analysts' forecasts. The analysts' forecasts may significantly depend on the accounting policies adopted by various companies, as different valuation and recognition models may lead to different properties of quality of the information environment.

In particular, investors, analysts and policy makers require credible accounting information to assess the real firm's economic performance and to take subsequently optimal decisions. Earnings are the primary information source for investors rather than any other performance indicators (such as dividend and cash flows). Hence, the main aim of earnings' reporting is to provide useful information for those people who have high interest in financial reports (Francis, LaFond, Olsson, & Schipper, 2004). One issue is whether accounting information of firms is able to cope satisfactorily with such a wide variety of needs. The other issue is that the users are by definition concerned with the future disposition of resources in making economic decisions. Users would therefore like to be provided with information which either predicts what is going to happen to the firm or enables them to make their own predictions using the accounting information.

Anyway, the volume of accounting earnings cannot be always a good criterion for investors' decision-making since sometimes earnings are manipulated by management. Hence, financial analysts have to note both the quantity and the quality of earnings. Quality of earnings is crucial for the well-functioning of markets, and it was put forward to help investors in making proper decisions. The reactions of investors to reported earnings are based upon the idea that high-quality earnings provide useful information for equity valuation. Therefore, when the quality of the information is high, there should be a tighter relationship between accounting information and investors' decisions.

Earnings quality (EQ) is an important aspect of evaluating an entity's financial health, and it is a significant summary characteristic of accounting systems. Although investors, creditors, and other financial statements' users often overlook it, EQ is lately becoming of considerable interest to participants in the financial reporting process (including Standard Setters, preparers, auditors, regulators, analysts, and financial press commentators) and to accounting researchers. In this context, researchers have proposed different measures of EQ, e.g., the value relevance of earnings, timeliness, conservatism, accruals quality, persistence, and predictability, among other measures. The fundamental differences among these measures are expected to make them differentially effective in capturing the multidimensional construct of EQ, as well as to be different approaches to the measurement of it. It is noted that in academic research, the empirical measures applied to assess EQ are likely to be sensitive to differences in firm-level economic circumstances and business models (Schipper & Vincent, 2003). According to Balsam, Krishnan, and Yang (2003), several measures of EQ exist in literature since different procedures capture the various manifestations and interpretations of EQ (Kirschenheiter & Melumad, 2002).

1.2 Earnings Quality: Background

The concept of EQ is a significant and critical issue attracting interest within the financial reporting process (Teets, 2002). The emphasis on EQ, as well as, on earnings management (EM) increased during the 1990s when the U.S. Securities and Exchange Commission (SEC) criticized managers and auditors. SEC accused managers to focus on opportunistic EM, and it suspected auditors to operate as managers' accomplices in deceiving the public. Managers had incentives to manage earnings and to meet capital market expectations due to the general importance of both firms' stock market valuations together and their stock-based compensations (Dechow & Skinner, 2000). SEC's criticism against managers and auditors made researchers more likely to study both issues related to how managers meet earnings targets and matters related to the role of audit quality in earnings reporting (DeFond, 2010).

Later, in the early of 2000s, big financial scandals in the USA and Europe broke out (e.g., Enron, WorldCom, Parmalat). During this period, EQ literature continued to grow as the consequence of these financial scandals even if the concerns regarding it existed since long before. In order to restore investors' confidence, the importance of financial reporting quality, with a special emphasis on EQ, was highlighted. In recent years, the quality of financial reporting and the quality of earnings have becoming a common subject in accounting research, as documented by the multiple literature that have reviewed the research on this topic (e.g., Dechow & Schrand, 2004; Demerjian, Lev, Lewis, & McVay, 2013; Gaio & Raposo, 2011; Gutiérrez & Rodríguez, 2019; Penman, 2003). Despite the increased attention on EQ and the big volume of the literature concerning it, yet the concept is not well defined.

The term "earnings quality" is vague and it is difficult to define. The literature on EQ currently embraces various aspects of this nebulous concept and no unique definition of it can be found. Evidence from prior research suggests that EQ is also a multidimensional concept (Gutiérrez & Rodríguez, 2019) that makes people consider quality of earnings differently. Referring to Teets (2002), "some consider quality of earnings to encompass the underlying economic performance of a firm, as well as the accounting statements that report on the underlying phenomenon, others consider quality of earnings to refer only to how well accounting earnings convey information about the underlying phenomenon". In this regard, Dechow and Schrand (2004) stated in their preface of EQ monograph that: "understanding a company's quality of earnings requires expertise in finance, accounting and corporate strategy and a strong knowledge of the industry in which the company operates and the governance mechanisms monitoring and rewarding employees and managers". Regardless of the definition of EQ, there are some factors on which might depend its meaning. Those factors include the special characteristics of firms' business model, the features of financial reporting system that firms implement, the expertise of auditors, or the goals and the incentives of managers when they make reporting choices.

Schipper and Vincent (2003) stated that: "although the phrase 'earnings quality' is widely used, there is neither a unique meaning assigned to the phrase nor a generally accepted approach to measuring earnings quality". Furthermore, Barker (2004) noted that no definition of earnings has been provided in the Financial Accounting Standard Board (FASB) Conceptual Framework,[1] which makes EQ difficult to interpret. Nevertheless, for the particular interest of this issue, the definition utilized by Dechow and Schrand (2004) is considered the most appropriate one to be adopted as it considers all the elements for high quality of earnings (i.e., persistence, predictability, and lack of variability) in one definition. The authors defined earnings to be of high quality when the earnings' number "is one that accurately reflects the company's current operating performance, is a good indicator of future operating performance, and is a useful summary measure for assessing firm value". The definition suggested that reported earnings are of high quality when they accurately reflect the firm's true earnings, they are helpful in predicting future performance, and they are a useful summary to evaluate the firm's current value.

The quality of earnings is usually defined in accounting studies from two different perspectives: the decision-usefulness perspectives and the economic-based perspectives. From a decision-usefulness perspective, EQ is regarded as being high if the earnings numbers are useful for decision-making purposes. Based on this point of view, the notion of EQ is defined differently by different users of financial statements. For example, according to Dechow and Schrand (2004), analysts are likely to view earnings to be of high quality when the earnings numbers accurately reflect the company's current operating performance, are good indicators of future operating performance, and are a good summary measure for assessing firm value. This is consistent with the objectives of financial analysts, which are the evaluation of the company performance, the assessment of the extent to which current earnings indicate future performance, and the judgment whether the current stock price reflects intrinsic firm value. On

[1] The Conceptual Framework (or "Concepts Statements") is a body of interrelated objectives and fundamentals. The objectives identify the goals and purposes of financial reporting and the fundamentals are the underlying concepts that help achieve those objectives. Those concepts provide guidance in selecting transactions, events, and circumstances to be accounted for, how they should be recognized and measured, and how they should be summarized and reported.

the other hand, creditors and compensation committees may define high-quality earnings as earnings that are easily convertible into cash flows and that reflect managers' real performance.

A variety of definitions and measurement criteria have been put forward for EQ depending on the information to be used to estimate it. The term "earnings quality" has no established meaning and has been used with different interpretations; it is a rather nebulous concept (Bellovary, Giacomino, & Akers, 2005; Cornell & Landsman, 2003; Schipper & Vincent, 2003). Hence, what are "high quality" earnings? The answer is not so simple. Numerous researchers stated various definitions of EQ in their studies.

1.3 Earnings Quality: Definitions

In literature, there is not an agreed-upon definition for EQ or a generally accepted approach for measuring it (Abdelghany, 2005; Schipper & Vincent, 2003). As capital markets rely on relevant and credible financial information, managers, accountants, auditors, Standard Setters, regulators are interested in EQ. In this regard, Teets (2002) stated that "higher quality earnings provide more information about the features of a firm's financial performance that are relevant to a specific decision made by a specific decision-maker". According to this definition, "quality" is conditional on specific decision context (Dechow, Ge, & Schrand, 2010) and it is a matter of subjective determination (Siegel, 1982). As EQ depends on the specific situation, its concept is conditional on the frame of reference. Moreover, EQ is contextual as it means different things to different financial statements' users. A possible explanation for the multiplicity of those different interpretations could be that different stakeholders use the information to make different decisions (Kirschenheiter & Melumad, 2002).

For example, investors use EQ "as a conditioning variable to extract valuation-relevant information from earnings patterns" (Francis, LaFond, Olsson, & Schipper, 2003). The financial press refers to fraudulent reporting as an "earnings quality" problem even if reported earnings and the related disclosure are in accordance with Generally Accepted Accounting Principles. Standard Setters, regulators, and auditors may disagree with the press on this point as they generally view earnings to be of high quality when they conform to the spirit and the rules identified in GAAPs and

IFRSs. In contrast, creditors are likely to view earnings to be of high quality when they are easily convertible into cash flows. Compensation committees otherwise are likely to view earnings to be of high quality when they reflect managers' real performance and they are little influenced by factors beyond management control. These examples illustrate that the decision-maker's objective and the role of earnings in the decision model drive the definition of EQ.

Dechow and Schrand (2004) provided a comprehensive and detailed review of the EQ research with numerous penetrating insights. Earnings are assumed to be of higher quality when they provide more information about the features of a firm's financial performance for decision-making (Dechow et al., 2010). The authors analyzed EQ from a financial analysis perspective, taking the view that earnings are of high quality if they "accurately annuitize the intrinsic value of the firm". They identify this value attribute with the reporting of a normalized, sustainable or representative earnings number that corresponds to permanent earnings. Moreover, they described earnings as being of high quality because they have three attributes: they accurately reflect current performance; they indicate future performance; and they are a useful summary for assessing firm value. EQ refers to the ability of reported earnings to reflect the company's true earnings, as well as the usefulness of reported earnings to predict future earnings.

The accounting literature embraces several definitions of EQ, and different studies focus on one or more aspects of earnings. Aspects often mentioned are the persistence, the informativeness and the sustainability of earnings. EQ also refers to the stability, predictability, and lack of variability of reported earnings. Lipe (1986), Kormendi and Lipe (1987) and Richardson (2003) viewed earnings to be of high quality when they are persistent. This interpretation focuses on the concept of persistence of earnings, where persistence is characterized by the ability to maintain earnings in the long term, or by having permanent rather than transitory earnings. EQ is the degree to which earnings' performance persists into the next period providing a good indication of future earnings. According to Kirschenheiter and Melumad (2002), earnings of high quality are those that are informative and close to the long-run value of the firm. In fact, a more general explanation of the persistence idea is suggested by tethering EQ with predictability, based on the assumption that earnings of high quality are a good indicator of future earnings. In particular, Penman and Zhang (2002), Dechow and Schrand (2004), and Melumad and Nissim (2009) defined earnings of high quality those that are persistent and hence the best predictor of future long-run sustainable earnings. Earnings are of high quality when they are sustainable. Sustainability means that earnings obtained through recurring activities are considered of better quality than those obtained through non-recurring activities. Hence, highly persistent earnings are viewed as sustainable and those that can be sustained for a long period of time can be labeled earnings of high quality.

The concept of informativeness is related to information content with respect to future earnings. Ball and Shivakumar (2005) interpreted the quality of earnings as information usefulness to investors, creditors, managers, and other parties. In this sense, Dechow and Schrand (2004) and Bellovary et al. (2005) defined EQ as the ability of reported earnings' numbers to reflect the company's true earnings as well as its usefulness to predict future earnings. To synthesize, earnings of high quality could be defined as earnings that are persistent, sustainable, and informative.

Earnings are also considered of high quality if they are predictable and easy to forecast. Prior literature defined earnings in terms of predictive ability of past earnings in predicting future ones (Lipe, 1990). For example, Schipper and Vincent (2003) considered earnings of high quality those that "predict future earnings better". Dechow et al. (2010), further, defined earnings of high quality those that are relevant to a specific decision made by a specific decision-maker because they provide more information about features of a firm's financial performance (Chen, Hemmer, & Zhang, 2007; Demerjian et al., 2013; Francis et al., 2004; Gaio & Raposo, 2011). More broadly, the quality of earnings' reporting refers to the ability of accounting earnings to signal future firm's cash flows In particular, Sloan (1996) and Dechow and Dichev (2002) claimed that earnings of high quality are those that "are backed by past, present or future cash flows".

Others defined EQ by relating to EM. In this regard, Brown (1999), Healy and Wahlen (1999), and Leuz, Nanda, and Wyscocki (2003) viewed earnings to be of higher quality when EM is low. Finally, some authors use the term "earnings quality" in the context of accounting conservatism. For example, White, Sondhi, and Fried (2003) and Penman and Zhang (2002) defined EQ as the amount of conservatism in a firm's reported earnings. Similarly, according to Watts (2003a, 2003b) earnings of high quality are those that "are derived under conservative accounting rules or the conservative application of relevant rules". Francis et al.

(2004) and Dechow and Schrand (2004) stated that smoothed earnings and those that do not have special or non-recurring items are earnings of high quality.

The measurement of EQ can be based on the relation between the most fundamental measures of firm's performance, i.e., cash flows and earnings. EQ is linked with how a firm's cash flows have been transformed into reported earnings. Hence, EQ is closely related to whether accruals are correctly used to transform cash flows into informative reported earnings (Mikhail, Walther, & Willis, 2003). In fact, in several studies, accruals and cash flows have been established as indicators of EQ. For example, Dechow and Dichev (2002) and Francis et al. (2004) considered EQ as the relationship between accruals and cash flow. Accruals play a crucial role in this transformation process, since cash flows come upon timing and matching issues which do not adequately reflect a firms' underlying financial performance. The magnitude of accruals in relation to earnings and cash flows is a well-established measure of EQ (Burgstahler, Hail, & Leuz, 2006) as a higher magnitude of accruals is associated with poorer EQ. According to DeAngelo (1986); Jones (1991); Dechow, Sloan, and Sweeney (1995); and Kothari, Leone, and Wasley (2005), earnings of high quality are those that "present smaller changes in total accruals that are not linked to fundamentals".

Some authors relate EQ to the accurate representation of underlying economic transactions and events. Hodge (2003) defines EQ as the degree to which reported net income differs from true earnings. Francis et al. (2003) suggested that EQ is used by investors "as a conditioning variable to extract valuation-relevant information from earnings patterns". Thus, EQ is interesting for future and current investors as well as for contracting purposes. EQ is the degree to which accounting figures more accurately represent the underlying economic fundamentals of the firm and the extent to which they map into operating cash flow realizations. Also, Chan, Chan, Jegadeesh, and Lakonishok (2006) consider EQ as the degree to which reported income reflects operating fundamentals and offer an accurate representation of underlying economic transactions and events. Therefore, EQ refers to how quickly and precisely reported earnings reveal fundamental earnings.

In this regard, Teets (2002) states that "some consider quality of earnings to encompass the underlying economic performance of a firm, as well as the accounting standards that report on that underlying phenomenon; others consider quality of earnings to refer only to how well accounting earnings convey information about the underlying phenomenon". Pratt (2000) defines EQ as "the extent to which net income reported on the income statement differs from true earnings". Our definition of EQ draws from Pratt's definition. We define EQ as the ability of reported earnings to reflect the company's true earnings and to predict future earnings. We examine the issue from the point of view of an analyst wishing to forecast future earnings. We interpret the term to mean that reported earnings, purged of transparently extraordinary items, is of good quality if it is a good indicator of future earnings. Thus, we have in mind the notion of "sustainable earnings" that is often referred to in financial analysis.

Our perspective also complements that taken by Dechow and Schrand (2004) as we associate EQ with precise (i.e., low variance) information about a construct that earnings are intended to describe; in the context of Dechow and Schrand's discussion, for example, this construct would be permanent earnings. Hence, high-quality earnings provide more information about the features of a firm's financial performance that are relevant to a specific decision made by a specific decision-maker. There are three features to note about the definition of EQ. First, EQ is conditional on the decision relevance of the information. Thus, under our definition, the term "earnings quality" alone is meaningless as it can be defined only in the context of a specific decision model. Second, the quality of reported earnings depends on whether it is informative about the firm's financial performance.

Third, EQ is jointly determined by the relevance of underlying financial performance to the decision and by the ability of the accounting system to measure performance. This definition of EQ suggests that quality could be evaluated with respect to any decision that depends on an informative representation of financial performance.

In this regard, some researchers focused on the concept of decision usefulness to express a definition of EQ. For example, Schipper and Vincent (2003) defined EQ as "the extent to which reported earnings faithfully represent Hicksian income".[2] Hence, the closer the earnings are to the Hicksian income, the higher the quality of earnings. To this point, we clarify that the Hicksian income is that income that "corresponds

[2] The Hicksian income (Hicks, 1939) is the maximum value a man can consume in a week and still be as well off at the end of the week as he was in the beginning. In other words, the Hicksian income is the maximum amount that can be consumed consistent with the maintenance of wealth.

to the amount that can be consumed (that is, the paid out dividends) during a period, while leaving the firm equally well off at the beginning and the end of the period" (Hicks, 1939). The term "faithfully representing" means the "correspondence or agreement between a measure or description and phenomenon that it purports to represent". The practical advantage of using the Hicksian income in order to explain the variation in the EQ constructs and measures is that it allows researchers to consider reported earnings even in the absence of accounting rules providing a neutral benchmark to observe EQ in this way.

The application of different concepts and definitions about EQ by researchers and analysts has led to the development of a variety of EQ measurement models. Each EQ model can be used for limited goals, and although each of these models uses different criteria, none of them gives a comprehensive perspective of EQ (Bellovary et al., 2005). Since no unique definition of EQ exists, a multitude of measures coexists. The empirical literature has developed several metrics to proxy EQ, including persistence, predictability, smoothness, abnormal accruals, accruals quality, value relevance, timeliness, conservatism, and others. Despite their widespread use, there is little theory offering explanations whether these metrics measure the same construct, different aspects of a construct, or different constructs; and whether they are substitutes or complements. Assuming that several metrics are complements, some studies aggregate them into an EQ score, usually by adding up the ranks of the metrics. Without a theoretical guidance, it is unclear how to interpret such compound metrics. Even though a vast stream of accounting research on EQ demonstrates its consequences on stock prices and returns (Callen, Khan, & Lu, 2013), cost of capital (Francis, Nanda, & Olsson, 2008), or information asymmetry (Bhattacharya, Desai, & Venkataraman, 2013), little is known about how EQ impacts on the accuracy of forecast models.

We focus on the use of earnings as a measure of company performance. Specifically, we take the position that a high-quality earnings number will do three things: It will reflect current operating performance; it will be a good indicator of future operating performance; and it will accurately annuitize the intrinsic value of the company. By considering all these descriptions, we should expect to have various approaches resulting in different assessments of EQ. In fact, based on a range of definitions of EQ, various constructs and measures of EQ have been developed by academic researchers. In the next chapter, five main attributes of earnings (persistence, predictability, variability/smoothness, discretionary accruals, and accrual quality) that are commonly used by researchers to construct and measure EQ are discussed.

High-quality earnings "provide more information about the features of firm's financial performance that are relevant to a specific decision made by a specific decision-maker" (Dechow et al., 2010). However, Dichev, Graham, Harvey, and Rajgopal (2013) performed a large-scale survey of chief officers (CFOs) and standard setters to provide new insights into the concept of EQ. Specifically, the interviewers asked CFOs to explain the perception of EQ. The results showed that a CFO's idea of EQ relates to earnings that are sustainable and repeatable. Specific accounting behaviors that positively affect the quality of earnings include, among others, consistent reporting choices over time, avoiding unreliable long-term estimates as much as possible, and backing earnings with cash flows. High-quality earnings persist, are free from one-time items, reflect long-term trends, and have the highest chance of being repeated in future periods.

1.4 Usefulness and Informativeness of Earnings Quality

The quality of financial reporting has been receiving special attention of those who use financial statements for contracting purposes and for investment decision-making (Schipper & Vincent, 2003). Security analysts, firm managers, and investors all devote a great deal of interest to firms' reported earnings. Especially investors search for the quality of financial reporting and reliable information regarding the company's financial condition. Investors pay a lot of attention to earnings for better assessing firm value and for making correct investment decisions (Gaio & Raposo, 2011). The investing public's needs and demands regarding the quality of financial reporting and the understanding of a company's financial condition have multiple aspects. These include—but certainly are not limited to—the quality of earnings, liquidity, strength of the balance sheet, and transparency of an enterprise's financial reporting, each of which, while intertwined, is a separate, complex subject.

According to Siegel (1982), financial analysts use earnings for making forecasts about the securities' future outcomes. Lev (2003) states that institutional investors and corporate boards are interested in earnings to value both the quality of management and the general firm's performance. Standard Setters view the quality of financial reports as an indirect feedback for assessing the quality of Financial Reporting

Standards (Schipper & Vincent, 2003) as the quality of financial reports results from the Accounting Standards used to develop the earnings figures.

Earnings are the main performance indicator as well as the main source of financial information in capital markets. That is, earnings are a good indicator of future cash flows and provide more useful information about a firm's economic performance than cash flows (Dechow, Kothari, & Watts, 1998). So, as earnings include information of great significance about a company's value, companies use them as their main means to inform stakeholders about firm-specific accounting and financial aspects (Wild, 1994).

More specifically, from the valuation point of view, as is already mentioned, earnings can be considered a summary measure of firm performance and one of the most essential accounting information that listed companies disclose to investors. In financial theory, the evaluation models often forecast and analyze a company's value based on accounting earnings. As a result, earnings are one of the most intuitive measures reflecting the business operating results for a certain period. Capital markets rely on relevant and credible financial accounting information, and earnings are widely considered as of high information content. Relevant information must have the ability to make a difference in different users' decision-making contexts when it is used by various users (Soderstrom & Sun, 2007). Credible information must give, as much as possible, a true, complete, unbiased, and free from errors representation of a firm's financial situation. Further, the quality of accounting information is strongly linked to how firm performance is measured as any improvement in the quality of accounting information should provide better tools for the valuation of the firm.

Dechow (1994) asserts that earnings are very important for a large variety of stakeholders and mainly investors and managers use earnings as one of the main guides to identify and evaluate investment opportunities (Bushman & Smith, 2003). In addition, investors use earnings to extract value-relevant information from the pattern of financial reporting (Francis et al., 2004). As investors rely on the quality of reported earnings for making decisions, high-quality and transparent financial reporting is vital to value securities and to inspire their confidence. On the contrary, false reported earnings can cause huge losses on their investment and could damage the economy as a whole through the undesirable effect of low-quality earnings (Pergola, 2005).

1.5 Earnings Quality and Financial Reporting

A major interest in financial reporting is EQ, which is part of the overall financial reporting quality. Using different approaches to define EQ, the extant literature emphasizes that the quality of earnings is very important to users of financial information as well as to practitioners, regulators, and accounting researchers. This is because reported earnings are considered to be the premier information in financial statements. The primary product of financial reporting is net income or earnings as a summary measure of firm performance for a wide range of users (e.g., for executive compensation plans or in debt covenants). Earnings are the summary measure of firm performance produced under the accrual basis of accounting. Another explanation for the prominence of accounting earnings is that they reflect cash flow forecasts and have a higher correlation with value than current cash flow. The inclusion of those forecasts causes earnings to be a better forecast of (and so a better proxy for) future cash flows than current ones. This is one of the reasons why earnings are often used in valuation models and as performance measures instead of operating cash flows.

Information asymmetry between management and other contracting parties creates a demand for an internally generated measure of firm performance over finite intervals. The success of a firm depends ultimately on its ability to generate cash receipts in excess of disbursements. Therefore, one performance measure that could be used is net cash receipts (realized cash flows). However, over finite intervals, reporting realized cash flows is not necessarily informative. This is because realized cash flows have timing and matching problems that cause them to be a "noisy" measure of firm performance. Accruals are used in financial reporting to overcome problems with measuring firm performance when firms are in continuous operation.

Generally Accepted Accounting Principles have evolved to enhance performance measurement by using accruals to alter the timing of cash flows recognition in earnings. Two important accounting principles that guide the production of earnings are the revenue recognition principle and the matching principle. By having such principles, the accrual process is hypothesized to mitigate timing and matching problems inherent in cash flows so that earnings more closely reflects firm performance (Dechow, 1994).

According to Salvato and Moores (2010), the high quality of accounting information on earnings is essential for firms to access equity and debt markets. EQ is a key characteristic of financial reporting as it embodies the principle that financial reports should be as useful as possible to investors and other capital providers in making their resource allocation decisions. High-quality financial reports should improve decision-making and, thus, capital market efficiency. However, EQ is an elusive construct and people tend to understand it in various different ways.

Amernic and Robb (2003) believed that the term "quality of earnings" should comprise more than the financial statement items. The authors included the general information setting into their definition of EQ as they believed that all the important players in the financial reporting process could have a significant influence over the financial reports.[3] Entwistle and Phillips (2003) suggest that EQ should be in line with the core purpose of financial reporting that is to provide relevance and reliability to financial statement users. In this regard, EQ reflects the usefulness and the relevance of earnings numbers.

To summarize, financial statements can be regarded as being of high quality when reported earnings accurately reflect underlying economic events and conditions as well as they enable financial statements' users to make better decisions. The perspective of decision usefulness is related to persistence and value relevance of the reported earnings (Jonas & Blanchet, 2000; Schipper & Vincent, 2003). Highly persistent earnings mean more permanent and less transitory values so that users of financial statements recognize them as earnings of high quality. Hung (2000) defined the value relevance of accounting information as the ability of financial statements to summarize information that affects firm value (Barth, Beaver, & Landsman, 2001; Schipper & Vincent, 2003). Thus, persistence and value relevance can be a good proxy of EQ reflecting the concept of decision usefulness.

The informative function of earnings means that it is often used as a basis for describing the financial performance of a firm. For example, the earnings figures and various ratios or metrics derived from them are widely used in compensation agreements and debt agreements. Earnings

[3] Amernic and Robb (2003) had put forward management as one entity that might affect the quality of earnings. Because management is one of the internal structures of the accounting entity, they might influence the quality of earnings from a variety of perspectives such as corporate culture and ethical climate.

are also used by analysts to evaluate firms' previous and current performance and to forecast firms' future ability to create additional wealth to shareholders. Earnings also provide the reader of financial reporting with enough information to facilitate an understanding of the various components of earnings, risks, and uncertainties that influence the future results of the company.

The standpoint of stewardship (or accountability) emphasizes financial information transparency, faithfulness and objectivity showing the important role that the quality of accounting information plays in reducing asymmetries between firms and investors (García-Teruel, Martínez-Solano, & Sánchez, 2009). Ball, Kothari, and Robin (2000) and Rezaee (2002) proposed that financial information should be fully and fairly disclosed and should not mislead or confuse users of the financial statements. Existing literature identifies several attributes of reported income that are widely considered to be desirable characteristics of a firm's reported earnings (Barton, Hansen, & Pownall, 2010; Francis et al., 2004).

One such attribute is EQ which is the aggregate result of the application of various accounting treatments, estimates, and assumptions that are made by management. Literature also finds that EQ is negatively associated with information asymmetry (Bhattacharya, Daouk, & Welker, 2003; Francis et al., 2004) and such an asymmetry could be expected to have an impact on the ability of analysts to predict earnings. Among other resources, analysts are known to rely on accounting information to develop earnings forecasts (Barker & Imam, 2008). Since reported financial accounting information is intended for external users and earnings are a "premier source" of such information, it is reasonable to assume that the quality of earnings could affect the decisions and the outcomes of financial statements' users. In summary, the role of financial reporting under the view of stewardship (or accountability) is to monitor management by mitigating information asymmetry between managers and stakeholders.

EQ based on stewardship (or accountability) can be measured by conservatism and accruals quality. Conservatism captures financial statement transparency since it constrains managerial opportunistic behavior and offsets managerial biases with its financial information asymmetry (Ball et al., 2000; Ball & Shivakumar, 2005; Watts, 2003a). Accruals quality is a good proxy of EQ (Schipper & Vincent, 2003) since it represents the faithfulness of financial reporting. For those assessing the quality of earnings, it is critical to understand that low quality of earnings is not necessarily indicative of poor financial reporting or of the misapplication of accounting policies, judgments, and estimates. Determining criteria of financial reporting quality are defined as a degree of aggressiveness or conservatism of accounting principles. The conflict of interests between information providers and investors, the estimation of some income components, the possibility of using different acceptable accounting methods and subjects like smoothing and EM, threaten the application of earnings as a criterion for decision-making. These circumstances double the necessity of studying EQ issue since it is very important that the reported earnings are high in quality.

The importance of EQ can be explained from at least two perspectives: the contracting perspective and the investment perspective. From the contracting perspective, low quality of earnings may result in unintentional wealth transfers. For instance, firms that rewards managers based on earnings may overcompensate the managers if earnings are overstated. From an investing perspective, poor quality of earnings is problematic as it can mislead investors, resulting in the misallocation of resources. High EQ would also increase the attractiveness of stocks to outside investors and market liquidity, lower cost of debt, reduce cost of capital (Leuz & Verrecchia, 2000; Young & Guenther, 2003) and promote more efficient capital allocation (Biddle, Hilary, & Verdi, 2009; Bushman & Smith, 2001).

Determining the quality of earnings is an essential part of the procedure of processing and interpreting information. Understanding a company's quality of earnings and its implication for firm value is complex and requires expertise in finance, accounting, corporate strategy, and a strong knowledge of the industry in which the company operates and the governance mechanisms that monitor and reward employees and managers. Some companies, by the nature of their business, will have low-quality earnings even in the absence of intentional earnings manipulation. Even accounting numbers that faithfully follow the spirit of GAAPs may not provide an earnings number that is a good indicator of future cash flows. In these cases, the current financial reporting model, rather than intentional EM or poor monitoring, is to blame for low-quality earnings. Thus, we begin by looking at EQ issues associated with the inherent strengths and weaknesses of the accrual accounting system for measuring performance. We leave an examination of the opportunities for purposeful manipulation of the earnings numbers for later chapters.

Bibliography

Abdelghany, K. E. (2005). Measuring the quality of earnings. *Managerial Auditing Journal, 20*(9), 1001–1015.

Aktas, R., & Kargin, S. (2012). Predictive ability of earnings and cash flows: Evidence from Turkish firms' cash flow statements that prepared by IAS 7. *Journal of Money, Investment and Banking, 25,* 171–180.

Amernic, J. H., & Robb, S. W. G. (2003). "Quality of earnings" as a framing device and unifying theme in intermediate financial accounting. *Issues in Accounting Education, 18*(1), 1–21.

Armstrong, C. S., Gyay, W. R., & Weber, J. P. (2010). The role of information and financial reporting in corporate governance and debt contracting. *Journal of Accounting and Economics, 50*(2–3), 179–234.

Ball, R., & Shivakumar, L. (2005). Earnings quality in UK private firms: Comparative loss recognition timeliness. *Journal of Accounting and Economics, 39*(1), 83–128.

Ball, R., Kothari, S. P., & Robin, A. (2000). The effect of international institutional factors on properties of accounting earnings. *Journal of Accounting and Economics, 29*(1), 1–51.

Balsam, S., Krishnan, J., & Yang, J. S. (2003). Auditor industry specialization and earnings quality. *Auditing: A Journal of Practice & Theory, 22*(2), 71–97.

Barker, R. (2004). Reporting financial performance. *Accounting Horizons, 18*(2), 157–172.

Barker, R., & Imam, S. (2008). Analysts' perceptions of "earnings quality". *Accounting and Business Research, 38*(4), 313–329.

Barth, M. E., Beaver, W. H., & Landsman, W. R. (2001). The relevance of the value relevance literature for financial accounting standard setting: Another view. *Journal of Accounting and Economics, 31*(1–3), 77–104.

Barton, J., Hansen, B., & Pownall, G. (2010). Which performance measures do investors around the world value the most and why? *Accounting Review, 85*(3), 753–789.

Bellovary, J. L., Giacomino, D. E., & Akers, M. D. (2005). Earnings quality: It's time to measure and report. *CPA Journal, 75*(11), 32–37.

Bhattacharya, U., Daouk, H., & Welker, M. (2003). The world price of earnings opacity. *The Accounting Review, 78*(3), 641–678.

Bhattacharya, N., Desai, H., & Venkataraman, K. (2013). Does earnings quality affect information asymmetry? Evidence from trading costs. *Contenporary Accounting Research, 30*(2), 482–516.

Biddle, G. C., Hilary, G., & Verdi, S. (2009). How does financial reporting quality relate to investment efficiency? *Journal of Accounting and Economics, 48*(2–3), 112–131.

Brown, P. R. (1999). Earnings management: A subtle (and troublesome) twist to earnings quality. *Journal of Financial Statement Analysis, 4*(2), 61–64.

Burgstahler, D. C., Hail, L., & Leuz, C. (2006). The importance of reporting incentives: Earnings management in European private and public firms. *The Accounting Review, 81*(5), 983–1016.
Bushman, R. M., & Smith, A. J. (2001). Financial accounting information and corporate governance. *Journal of Accounting and Economics, 32,* 237–333.
Bushman, R. M., & Smith, A. J. (2003). Transparency, financial accounting information, and corporate governance. *Economic Policy Review, 9*(1), 65–87.
Callen, J. L., Khan, M., & Lu, H. (2013). Accounting quality, stock price delay, and future stock returns. *Contemporary Accounting Research, 30*(1), 269–295.
Chan, K., Chan, L., Jegadeesh, N., & Lakonishok, J. (2006). Earnings quality and stock returns. *The Journal of Business, 79*(3), 1041–1082.
Chen, Q., Hemmer, T., & Zhang, Y. (2007). On the relation between conservatism in accounting standards and incentives for earnings management. *Journal of Accounting Research, 45*(3), 541–565.
Cornell, B., & Landsman, W. R. (2003). Accounting valuation: Is earnings quality an issue? *Financial Analysts Journal, 59*(6), 20–28.
DeAngelo, L. (1986). Accounting numbers as market valuation substitutes: A study of management buyouts of public stockholders. *The Accounting Review, 61*(3), 400–420.
Dechow, P. M. (1994). Accounting earnings and cash flows as measures of firm performance: The role of accounting accruals. *Journal of Accounting and Economics, 18*(1), 3–42.
Dechow, P. M., & Dichev, I. D. (2002). The quality of accruals and earnings: The role of accrual estimation errors. *The Accounting Review, 77*(Supplement), 35–59.
Dechow, P. M., Ge, W., & Schrand, C. (2010). Understanding earnings quality: A review of the proxies, their determinants and their consequences. *Journal of Accounting and Economics, 50*(2–3), 344–401.
Dechow, P. M., Kothari, S. P., & Watts, R. L. (1998). The relation between earnings and cash flows. *Journal of Accounting and Economics, 25*(2), 133–168.
Dechow, P. M., & Schrand, C. M. (2004). *Earnings quality.* Charlottesville, VA: United States of America: Research Foundation of CFA Institute.
Dechow, P. M., & Skinner, D. J. (2000). Earnings management: Reconciling the views of accounting academics, practitioners, and regulators. *Accounting Horizons, 14*(2), 235–250.
Dechow, P. M., Sloan, R. G., & Sweeney, A. P. (1995). Detecting earnings management. *The Accounting Review, 70*(2), 193–225.
DeFond, L. M. (2010). Earnings quality research: Advances, challenges and future research. *Journal of Accounting and Economics, 50*(2–3), 402–409.
Demerjian, P. R., Lev, B., Lewis, M. F., & McVay, S. E. (2013). Managerial ability and earnings quality. *The Accounting Review, 88*(2), 463–498.

Dichev, I. D., Graham, J. R., Harvey, C. R., & Rajgopal, S. (2013). Earnings quality: Evidence from the field. *Journal of Accounting and Economics, 56*(2–3), 1–33.

Entwistle, G. M., & Phillips, F. (2003). Relevance, reliability, and the earnings quality debate. *Issues in Accounting Education, 18*(1), 79–92.

Francis, J., LaFond, R., Olsson, P. M., & Schipper, K. (2003, April). Earnings quality and the pricing effects of earnings patterns. *SSRN Electronic Journal*, 1–52.

Francis, J., LaFond, R., Olsson, P. M., & Schipper, K. (2004). Costs of equity and earnings attributes. *The Accounting Review, 79*(4), 967–1010.

Francis, J., Nanda, D., & Olsson, P. (2008). Voluntary disclosure, earnings quality, and cost of capital. *Journal of Accounting Research, 46*(1), 53–99.

Gaio, C., & Raposo, C. C. (2011). Earnings quality and firm valuation: International evidence. *Accounting & Finance, 51*(2), 467–499.

García-Teruel, P. J., Martínez-Solano, P., & Sánchez, J. P. (2009). Accruals quality and corporate cash holdings. *Accounting & Finance, 49*(1), 95–115.

Gutiérrez, A. L., & Rodríguez, M. C. (2019). A review on the multidimensional analysis of earnings quality. *Spanish Accounting Review, 22*(1), 41–60.

Healy, P. M., & Wahlen, J. M. (1999). A review of the earnings management literature and its implications for standard setting. *Accounting Horizons, 13*(4), 365–383.

Hicks, J. R. (1939). *Value and capital: An inquiry into some fundamental principles of economic theory* (2nd ed.). Ely House, London: Oxford University Press.

Hodge, F. D. (2003). Investors' perceptions of earnings quality, auditor independence, and the usefulness of audited financial information. *Accounting Horizons, 17*(Suppl.), 37–48.

Hung, M. (2000). Accounting standards and value relevance of financial statements: An international analysis. *Journal of Accounting and Economics, 30*(3), 401–420.

Jonas, G. J., & Blanchet, J. (2000). Assessing quality of financial reporting. *Accounting Horizons, 14*(3), 353–363.

Jones, J. (1991). Earnings management during import relief investigations. *Journal of Accounting Research, 29*(2), 193–228.

Kirschenheiter, M., & Melumad, N. (2002). Can "big bath" and earnings smoothing co-exist as equilibrium financial reporting strategies? *Journal of Accounting Research, 40*(3), 761–796.

Kormendi, R., & Lipe, R. (1987). Earnings innovations, earnings persistence, and stock returns. *The Journal of Business, 60*(3), 323–345.

Kothari, S. P., Leone, A., & Wasley, C. E. (2005). Performance matched discretionary accruals measures. *Journal of Accounting and Economics, 39*(1), 163–197.

Leuz, C., Nanda, D., & Wyscocki, P. D. (2003). Earnings management and investor protection: An international comparison. *Journal of Financial Economics, 69*(3), 505–527.

Leuz, C., & Verrecchia, R. E. (2000). The economic consequences of increased disclosure. *Journal of Accounting Research, 38*(Supplement), 91–124.

Lev, B. (2003). Corporate earnings: Facts and fiction. *Journal of Economic Perspectives, 17*(2), 27–50.

Lipe, R. C. (1986). The information contained in the components of earnings. *Journal of Accounting Research, 24, Studies on Alternative Measures of Accounting Income, 24,* 37–64.

Lipe, R. C. (1990). The relation between stock returns and accounting earnings given alternative information. *The Accounting Review, 65*(1), 49–71.

Melumad, N. D., & Nissim, D. (2009). Line-item analysis of earnings quality. *Foundation and Trends in Accounting, 3*(2–3), 87–221.

Mikhail, M. B., Walther, B. R., & Willis, R. H. (2003). Reactions to dividend changes conditional on earnings quality. *Journal of Accounting, Auditing & Finance, 18*(1), 121–151.

Peek, E. (2005). The influence of accounting changes on financial analysts' forecast accuracy and forecasting superiority: Evidence from the Netherlands. *European Accounting Review, 14*(2), 261–295.

Penman, S. (2003). The quality of financial statements: Perspectives from the recent stock market bubble. *Accounting Horizons, 17*(1), 77–96.

Penman, S. H., & Zhang, X.-J. (2002). Accounting conservatism, the quality of earnings, and stock returns. *The Accounting Review, 77*(2), 237–264.

Pergola, T. M. (2005). Management entrenchment: Can it negate the effectiveness of recently legislated governance reform? *Journal of American Academy of Business, 6*(2), 177–183.

Pratt, J. (2000). *Financial accounting in an economic context* (4th ed.). Cincinnati, OH: South-Western College Publishing.

Rezaee, Z. (2002). *Financial statement fraud: Prevention and detection.* New York: Wiley.

Richardson, S. (2003). Earnings quality and short sellers. *Accounting Horizons, 17*(s-1), 49–61.

Salvato, C., & Moores, K. (2010). Research on accounting in family firms: Past accomplishments and future challenges. *Family Business Review, 23*(3), 193–215.

Schipper, K., & Vincent, L. (2003). Earnings quality. *Accounting Horizons, 17* (s-1), 97–110.

Siegel, J. G. (1982). The "quality of earnings" concept: A survey. *Financial Analysts Journal, 38*(2), 60–68.

Sloan, R. (1996). Do stock prices fully reflect information in accruals and cash flows about future earnings? *The Accounting Review, 71*(3), 289–315.

Soderstrom, N. S., & Sun, K. J. (2007). IFRS adoption and accounting quality: A review. *European Accounting Review, 16*(4), 675–702.

Teets, R. W. (2002). Quality of earnings: An introduction to the issues in accounting education special issue. *Issues in Accounting Education, 17*(4), 335–360.

Watts, R. (2003a). Conservatism in accounting, part I: Explanations and implications. *Accounting Horizons, 17*(3), 207–221.

Watts, R. (2003b). Conservatism in accounting, part II: Evidence and research opportunities. *Accounting Horizons, 17*(4), 287–301.

White, G. I., Sondhi, A. C., & Fried, H. D. (2003). *The analysis and use of financial statements* (3rd ed.). New York: Wiley.

Wild, J. J. (1994). Managerial accountability to shareholders: Audit committees and the explanatory power of earnings for returns. *The British Accounting Review, 26*(4), 353–374.

Young, D., & Guenther, D. A. (2003). Financial reporting environments and international capital mobility. *Journal of Accounting Research, 41*(3), 553–579.

CHAPTER 2

Measures of Earnings Quality

Abstract Earnings quality (EQ) has attracted special attention from researchers and their efforts have been to achieve a valid and reasonable method to assess it. In literature, there have been developed various definitions of EQ and have been proposed several approaches to measure it. Actually, there is no a generally accepted approach to measure EQ and empirical researchers use different empirical proxies that are likely related to desirable properties of accounting information. Although the existing plethora of acceptable methods for EQ measurement, none of these measures has revealed superior because EQ is considered a multidimensional concept that allows different users to interpret it differently. Therefore, the choice of an EQ measure depends on the research question posed and the availability of data and estimation models.

Keywords Earnings quality (EQ) · Measures · Earnings attributes · Conservatism · Accruals

2.1 Introduction

In the last few decades, earnings quality (EQ) has become one of the most important accounting research topics, and it has received more and more attention from investors, regulators as well as researchers. For example, some empirical studies analyzed EQ and their determinants over

E. Menicucci, *Earnings Quality*,
https://doi.org/10.1007/978-3-030-36798-5_2

time; others measured the effects of specific changes in Accounting Standards, enforcement systems, or corporate governance requirements on EQ within or across countries. The heightened attention to the subject of EQ is partly due to the wave of accounting scandals of the early 2000s (manipulation of accounting numbers).

The subject of EQ is a complex topic and no researcher has thus far been able to provide a unique definition of this concept. According to Balsam, Krishnan, and Yang (2003), there exist various measures of EQ in literature but those different proxies capture various manifestations of EQ. Moreover, there is neither a unique meaning of EQ nor a generally accepted approach to measuring it (Schipper & Vincent, 2003). EQ is considered a multidimensional concept that is difficult to measure and recent empirical research evaluates it by considering various earnings attributes (Dechow, Ge, & Schrand, 2010; Francis, LaFond, Olsson, & Schipper, 2004; Gaio, 2010; Kousenidis, Ladas, & Negakis, 2013). Since there is a variety of definitions and there is no a generally accepted measure of EQ, the literature has developed a number of measurement proxies, which focus on particular attributes of EQ (Khaled, 2005). Although there are no definitive criteria by which to evaluate EQ, most of them are based on intuitive and plausible concepts regarding the desirable characteristics of an accounting system. We comprise four characteristics of reported earnings that are expected to increase its usefulness for the decision-making process: absence of EM, earnings smoothness, time-series properties of earnings, and conservatism. This makes the choice of the appropriate measure a critical research design issue that is likely to have a significant effect on the evaluation results. Unfortunately, there is little guidance on how good the proxies for EQ really are and what might be the best measure in any given circumstances. In this chapter, we discuss the usefulness and the appropriateness of commonly used earnings metrics and we examine how these measures fulfill the objective of improving the decision usefulness of financial reports, i.e., how good their quality is. We also discuss how the time-series properties of earnings can be used as measures of EQ.

2.2 Measurement of Earnings Quality

Previous studies defined EQ referring to certain characteristics of earnings, such as persistence, sustainability, predictive ability, smoothness, conservatism, value relevance, timeliness, earnings management (or earnings manipulation) (EM), and accrual quality. In general, high-quality earnings are those that have a higher degree of persistence, lower grade of EM, and/or higher accrual quality are more predictable, less volatile, and more timely. In recent three decades, EQ has attracted special attention from researchers and their efforts have been to achieve a valid and reasonable method to assess EQ and its decisive factors. Thus, the proper selection of the criteria is an effective and essential issue affecting the results of researches.

Despite the concept "earnings quality" is widely used in literature, there is no consensus about one common definition (Teets, 2002) or a generally accepted approach for measuring it (Schipper & Vincent, 2003). In literature, there have been formulated various definitions and have been proposed several approaches to measure EQ, that capture different aspects of this multidimensional concept. Since EQ is directly unobservable, researchers use different empirical proxies that are expected to be associated with desirable properties of accounting information (Perotti & Wagenhofer, 2014). Versatility of definitions in this regard leads to a plethora of acceptable methods for EQ measurement. Anyway, none of these measures has revealed superior because EQ is considered a multidimensional concept that allows different users to interpret it differently. Therefore, the choice of an EQ measure depends on the research question posed (which dimension of EQ is implied by the research question) and the availability of data and estimation models (which measures can be estimated).

We found that most of empirical studies analyzed one of the characteristics of earnings. Furthermore, the research on the relationships among the different EQ dimensions is limited and conclusions are mixed. Finally, only a few studies use a multidimensional measure of EQ according to its various earnings properties (Leuz & Wysocki, 2016). Differences among varied criteria for EQ can anyhow help users of financial statements to judge about reliability and predictability of earnings. Some research questions call for a measure of EQ that is linked to investors' perceptions of earnings. For example, research that examines the value relevance of earnings presumes its usefulness to a particular class of market participants (namely investors) whose aggregate judgments (Ferrer, Callao, Jarne, & Lainez, 2016). In short, we can assess the usefulness of high quality of earnings from the viewpoints of financial information users, investors, and accounting standards regulators. In this respect, the term "quality" is seen as the usefulness of financial statements to investors, managers, creditors, and third parties contracting with the firm.

Our focus is on EQ from the perspective of the analyst. The objectives of financial analysis are to evaluate the performance of the company, to assess the extent to which current performance is indicative of future performance and to determine whether the current stock price reflects intrinsic firm value. From this perspective, a high-quality earnings number is one that accurately reflects the company's current operating performance, is a good indicator of future operating performance, and is a useful summary measure for assessing firm value. Hence, we define earnings to be of high quality when they accurately annuitize the intrinsic value of the firm. Quality of earnings is relative and covers a spectrum so that it is an oversimplification to refer to EQ as "good" versus "bad", or even "high" versus "low". There are many characteristics affecting the quality of earnings that can be considered by financial statements' users in evaluating particular earnings components.

We select some EQ measures that are commonly used in literature. Several possible constructs are based on a range of definitions of EQ and, as already mentioned above, are related to the time-series properties of earnings, which include persistence, predictability, and variability (Kormendi & Lipe, 1987).

2.3 Earnings Attributes

The main difficulty in discussing EQ is the presence of a large number of measures that have been used in literature since there is not a generally accepted approach to measure it. Previous studies about EQ have used different measures to approach EQ (DeAngelo, 1986; Dechow & Dichev, 2002; Dechow, Sloan, & Sweeney, 1995; Jones, 1991; Richardson, Sloan, Soliman, & Tuna, 2005; Schipper & Vincent, 2003; Sloan, 1996). In particular, there are generally four different constructs for EQ to derive its measures.

The first category refers to time-series properties of earnings. This construct looks at how EQ can be derived from the three major properties of earnings, namely persistence, predictability, and variability. These three properties are not mutually exclusive; for example, more variable earnings are less persistent and often less predictable, while highly persistent earnings are more predictable. The notion of predictability is also used in the conceptual framework of the IASB, as we will see later on. Variability of earnings is sometimes used as a measure of EQ as it indicates high quality of earnings when there is little volatility or there are smooth earnings.

However, earnings smoothing, by others, is related to EM, which would indicate lower quality of earnings (e.g., Leuz, Nanda, & Wyscocki, 2003). The second construct derives from the relations among cash, accruals, and income. These types of measures are also often used to determine the extent or the presence of EM. The third construct looks at how EQ measures derive from the qualitative concepts of the FASB Conceptual Framework that assesses quality in terms of relevance, reliability, and comparability/consistency.

Those three concepts cannot be separately measured. There is often a trade-off between one attribute and another and this trade-off is a subjective matter. Another problem is the importance that has to be placed on the term "comparability" (e.g., must comparability be achieved at the expense of relevance?). Finally, the fourth category is derived from implementation decisions. This actually goes back to the notion of EM and the effect of management decisions on the quality of earnings as indicated by Teets (2002). There are two decision types that affect EQ: First, the amount of required estimates implied by the type of Accounting Standards used and the second is the extent to which the management takes advantage where judgments or estimates have to be made. These four constructs interact with and overlap each other; for example, measures based on qualitative characteristics can be the same ones of those derived from time series. In this regard, some accruals-based measures are furthermore used to determine the amount of EM from implementation decisions.

The criteria used for EQ measurement can be classified into two categories: market-based and accounting-based (Francis, LaFond, Olsson, & Schipper, 2003). Market-based measures include value relevance, conservatism, and timeliness. The criteria used for these characteristics are based on the estimated relationships between accounting earnings and market return or market prices. Accounting-based measures include accruals quality, predictability, smoothing, and persistence; these characteristics are assessed using information on cash, earnings, and accruals.

Some previous researches suggest that accounting-based criteria have more explanatory power compared to market-based ones (Francis et al., 2004), while others show that the use of market-based criteria (e.g., earnings reaction coefficient—ERC[1]—and relevance) leads to more return and explanatory power compared to accounting-based ones (e.g., accruals quality or abnormal accruals) (Ewert & Wagenhofer, 2010). Prior literature also found that earnings consistency is a useful indicator to reveal EQ (Peterson, Schmardebeck, & Wilks, 2015), while predictability and income smoothing cannot represent EQ because they have not a uniform correspondence with informative content or reported earnings. The existence of these contradictions shows that there is a little overlap among different EQ measurement indices which in turn leads to contradictory and conflicting research results (Dechow et al. (2010); Francis et al., 2004).

We measure EQ using accounting-based attributes that do not depend on market perceptions (Burgstahler, Hail, & Leuz, 2006; Francis et al., 2004; Gaio, 2010; Kousenidis et al., 2013; Leuz et al., 2003). Among the accounting-based attributes, time-series properties of earnings indicate how profits are distributed over time and the statistical characteristics of the process that generates earnings. The time-series properties of earnings are affected by the volatility of operations, the economic environment, and the accounting systems employed (e.g., FVA).

Specifically, we consider the following earnings attributes: the persistence of earnings, which captures the extent to which a given innovation produces future earnings; the predictive ability of earnings, which is a function of the distribution of the innovation series; and the variability of earnings, which measures the time-series variance of innovations directly. Additionally, we include earnings smoothness which measures the intentional attempts of managers to eliminate fluctuations in earnings. Different EQ measurement methods lead to diverse assessments of it and companies cannot be judged as having poor or high EQ by using only one method. Therefore, stakeholders should select more than one method for assessing EQ before any investment decision-making.

Despite the widespread use of several metrics, there is no agreement on them, i.e., whether a high value of the metric indicates high or low EQ.

[1]The earnings response coefficient (ERC) is the stock market reaction (the change in stock price) for one unit of unexpected earnings. This can be measured around the earnings announcement (event study), or over a longer period, for example, a year. In financial economics and accounting, the ERC is the estimated relationship between equity returns and the unexpected portion of (i.e., new information in) companies' earnings announcements.

Therefore, some studies use the neutral term "earnings attributes" rather than EQ metrics. The metrics capture only certain aspects that are considered important for EQ, e.g., the time series of earnings or market price reactions on earnings. Therefore, many empirical studies aggregate several metrics into an EQ score, often by adding up the ranks of the included metrics. Dichev, Graham, Harvey, and Rajgopal (2013) observed that research on EQ defines high-quality earnings as those that are persistent, derive from conservative accounting rules, or reflect a conservative application of relevant rules, are smooth, are supported by cash flows and accurately predict future earnings.

In this regard, we have drawn only broad conclusions about the literature taken as a whole. We now provide a discussion of the specific proxies for EQ and in particular we debate a category of them: properties of earnings. To date, the quality of accounting information cannot be measured by a single variable. When considering the various properties of the accounting information, we can highlight those that are the most researched. Several studies, such as that conducted by Barth, Landsman, and Lang (2008), suggest that these properties may be directly related to each other and that one can affect the other. The following subsections discuss each of these measures, which have frequently been used in prior studies.

2.3.1 Earnings Persistence

EQ is defined in previous studies and accounting textbooks in terms of persistence and sustainability (e.g., Penman & Zhang, 2002; Richardson, 2003; Richardson et al., 2005; Sloan, 1996). Earnings persistence measures the degree to which current-period earnings shocks persist in the future and affects future earnings' expectations (Chen, Folsom, Paek, & Sami, 2014; Donnelly, 2002; Krishnan & Zhang, 2019). Hence, persistent earnings are current earnings that are likely to be maintained in the future. Earnings persistence is associated with stability, sustainability, and recurrence of earnings over time. Earnings persistence could be also defined as the systematic behavior of earnings and in this perspective persistent earnings are viewed as desirable because they are recurring. More specifically, persistence is often discussed in the context of sustainable or core earnings. Investors always view highly persistent earnings numbers as sustainable and prior research has interpreted the relation between a firm's reported earnings and its stock return as a measure of earnings persistence. Hence, high-quality earnings are sustainable, where the term "sustainable" is used as a synonym of "persistent" (Schipper & Vincent, 2003).

Based on theoretically and empirically demonstrated studies which show that there is a positive relationship between earnings persistence and the association between returns and earnings, earnings that are more persistent are viewed as of higher quality and more desirable.

Focusing on investors' perception of EQ, earnings are considered to be of high quality when they are sustainable. Hence, quality of earnings is the extent to which we might expect the reported earnings to be sustained (Bodie, Kane, & Marcus, 2002; Revsine, Collins, & Johnson, 2002). Similarly, Penman and Zhang (2002) defined high-quality earnings as "sustainable earnings" and according to them, when an accounting treatment produces unsustainable earnings, it indicates that the earnings figures are of poor quality.

Earnings persistence is measured as the slope coefficient from autoregressive models of earnings as follows. This measure, based on Lipe (1990), has been utilized by most researchers studying earnings persistence (Dichev & Tang, 2008; Francis et al., 2004; Gaio, 2010; Kousenidis et al., 2013).

$$X_{i,t} = \beta_0 + \beta_{1,i} X_{1,t-1} + \varepsilon_{1,t} \tag{2.1}$$

where $X_{i,t}$ and $X_{i,t-1}$ are firm i's earnings in year t and $t-1$, respectively, and coefficient $\varepsilon_{i,t}$ captures firm i's persistence of earnings.

Consequently, persistence measure (PERS) is derived from Eq. (2.1) as negative value of slope coefficient estimate:

$$\text{PERS}_i = -\beta_1$$

Values of slope coefficient β_1 close to 1 imply highly persistent earnings, while values of coefficient β_1 close to 0 imply highly transitory earnings (Francis et al., 2004). In order to transform this variable to our earnings attributes, we use the negative value of coefficient β_1. Thus, high values of PERS indicate low level of earnings persistence.

Firms differ in earnings informativeness and EQ because of differences in their degrees of earnings persistence since investors prefer earnings to be more stable rather than those exhibiting shocks (especially for risk-averse investors).

As demonstrated in prior literature (Lipe, 1990), earnings informativeness of a firm varies positively with earnings persistence and, in particular, earnings informativeness is positively related to the ability of past earnings to predict future earnings (i.e., earnings persistence). Explicitly, if the earnings innovation is likely to persist in future earnings, then the present value of revisions in future earnings is larger. High persistence is positively associated with high EQ, since it indicates a stable, sustainable and less volatile earnings' generation process that is particularly valued by investors. Up to this point, we have focused on earnings persistence studies that are motivated by the maintained assumption that more persistent earnings are indicative of higher EQ.

Earnings that represent the annuity of expected future cash flows are likely to be both persistent and predictable. Persistence and predictability of earnings, however, are not sufficient to indicate that earnings are of high quality.[2] Managers often want earnings to be highly persistent and predictable because these characteristics can improve their reputations with analysts and investors. Anyway, persistence alone is not indicative of high-quality earnings as the earnings stream must also reflect underlying intrinsic value. Non-persistent earnings may be caused by the normal application of Accounting Standards in some economic environments. Intervention from the management in the financial reporting process can transform non-persistent earnings into persistent earnings. Greater earnings persistence is a meaningful definition for EQ if earnings truly reflect performance during the period and if current-period performance persists in future periods.

2.3.2 *Earnings Predictability*

A number of studies measure EQ by assessing the ability of earnings to predict future earnings or cash flows (Barragato & Markelevich, 2008; Doyle, Lundholm, & Soliman, 2003; Francis et al., 2004; Van der Meulen, Gaeremynck, & Willekens, 2007). Predictive value explicitly refers to the firm's ability to generate future cash flows and in particular: "information about an economic phenomenon has predictive value if it has value as an input to predictive processes used by capital providers to

[2] Anctil and Chamberlain (2005) discussed how some accounting rules, such as depreciation treatment, can increase persistence but reduce the usefulness of current earnings as a measure of permanent earnings.

form their own expectations about the future" (IASB, 2010). For example, Barragato and Markelevich (2008) defined high-quality earnings as an earnings stream that is a good predictor of future operating cash flows.

Analysts usually associate high EQ with near-term earnings predictability that has been defined by many researchers as "the ability of past earnings to predict future earnings" (Cornell & Landsman, 2003; Francis et al., 2004; Lipe, 1990; Schipper & Vincent, 2003). We consider predictive value as the most important indicator of value relevance in terms of decision usefulness and we measure it using three items. The first item refers to the extent of forward-looking statements in annual reports. Forward-looking information usually describes management's expectations of the company for future years. For capital providers and other users of the annual report, this information is relevant since management has access to private information to produce a forecast that is not available to other stakeholders (Bartov & Mohanram, 2004).

The second item measures to what extent the annual report discloses information in terms of business opportunities and risks. We refer to the complementation of financial information by non-financial information and the knowledge that can be obtained about business opportunities, risks, and possible future scenarios for the company.

The third item measures company's use of Fair Value. Prior literature usually refers to the use of Fair Value versus Historical Cost when discussing the predictive value[3] of financial reporting information (Hirst, Hopkins, & Wahlen, 2004; McDaniel, Martin, & Maines, 2002; Schipper, 2003; Schipper & Vincent, 2003). It is often claimed that Fair Value Accounting (FVA) provides more relevant information than Historical Cost Accounting (HCA) because it represents the current value of assets, instead of the purchase price. Both the Financial Accounting Standard Board (FASB) and International Accounting Standard Board (IASB) have allowed more FVA to increase the relevance of financial reporting, since they consider Fair Value as one of most important methods to increase relevance.

[3]In addition to predictive value, confirmatory value contributes to the relevance of financial reporting information. Information has confirmatory value if it confirms or changes past (or present) expectations based on previous evaluations. Jonas and Blanchet (2000) claimed that if the information in the annual report provides feedback to the users of the annual report about previous transactions or events, this will help them to confirm or change their expectations.

Similar to persistence, predictability is viewed as a desirable attribute of earnings because it increases the accuracy of assessing the amounts, timing and uncertainties of earnings' forecasts and future cash flows. Predictability captures the notion that earnings are of higher quality the more useful they are in predicting future earnings. Bearing this in mind, predictive ability of earnings is linked to their decision usefulness, i.e., they can be considered as more useful if they accurately predict future cash flows. Predictability is also reflected in the variance of stock changes during the announcement of earnings. From this measurement perspective, earnings predictability is based on the variance of earnings shocks, where higher variance implies lower predictability. As the earnings predictability increases, the absolute magnitude of the earnings shock becomes smaller leading to a lower variance of price changes. Decrease in variance makes current earnings' information more useful in predicting future earnings, and, therefore, this reduction improves the predictability of earnings and its association with higher EQ.

Additionally, predictability is a conjunctive variable of the quality of both financial reporting and accounting system that measures it. Then, predictability influences the quality of financial reporting, which determines the quality of the accounting system but, at the same time, the quality of the accounting system also determines financial reporting quality. This predictability is defined in an economic sense in terms of a low level of earnings volatility and in an accounting sense in terms of management prudence in the establishment and adjustment of certain conservative reserves, allowances and off-balance-sheet assets (Bricker, Previts, Robinson, & Young, 1995).

The assessment of predictive ability is complicated due to the fact that the ability of earnings to predict itself might well increase by management involvement to smooth the reported series relative to the unreported unmanaged series. There are various arguments that current earnings may not be a good predictor of future cash flows compared to current cash flows because of the managerial discretion involved in measuring earnings. To clarify this matter, earnings predictability is a similar construct to earnings persistence as both relate to the time-series behavior of earnings.

However, there is a possible situation where persistence and predictability may not be consistent.[4]

As predictability (PRED) measures the ability of earnings to be predicted, this measure is based on the variance of the earnings shocks, where higher variance implies lower predictability. We use the square root of estimated error from Eq. (2.1).[5]

$$\mathrm{PRED}_i = \sqrt{\sigma^2 \varepsilon_{i,t}}$$

Large (small) values of predictability imply less (more) predictable earnings. Earnings that are more predictable are considered higher quality earnings. The use of predictability to measure EQ has been criticized for not accurately reflecting the quality of earnings. As earnings are often subjected to manipulation, persistence and predictability are not sufficient to indicate that earnings are of high quality (Dechow & Schrand, 2004). Managers can try to make earnings highly predictable by manipulation in order to improve their reputations with analysts and investors. Furthermore, the ability to forecast is often limited to the business model and economic situations that make cyclical and growing firms' earnings difficult to predict.

2.3.3 *Earnings Variability and Earnings Smoothness*

Variability (volatility) is the third earnings' attribute based on time-series property of earnings (Clubb & Wu, 2014). It is assumed that less volatile earnings are more predictable and persistent. In fact, another common proxy for earnings predictability is the variance of earnings: A higher variance is indicative of lower earnings predictability. Managers may introduce short-term components to the income series in order to decrease time-series variability and increase predictability. Variability is often associated with low quality of earnings since it is related to temporary variations of net income which do not represent the current value of the business

[4] Volatile earnings might be of high quality in terms of high persistence (i.e., earnings follows random walk), but low in quality in terms of low predictability (i.e., the magnitude of a typical shock to earnings is large).

[5] Earnings predictability has been measured with this method, proposed initially by Lipe (1990) and then by many researchers such as Francis et al. (2004), Gaio (2010), and Kousenidis et al. (2013), among others.

and the risk profile of the firm. On the contrary, absence of variability is related to high quality of earnings. One approach for assessing EQ is to test if income is inherently smooth or, in other words, if management has engaged in smoothing practices. Income smoothing is a technique used by managers to reduce the variability of the reported amount of income by means of artificial or real EM. Income smoothing practice is an attempt to report stable earnings as managers believe that smooth earnings are more highly valued, minimize the risk of possible debt and dividend covenant violation and can maximize management bonuses. Income smoothing can consist in using deceptive accounting techniques to level out fluctuations in net income from one period to the next. Companies indulge in this practice because investors are generally willing to pay a premium for stocks with steady and predictable earnings streams. In contrast, earnings that are subjected to more volatile patterns can be regarded as riskier. Examples of income smoothing techniques include deferring revenue during a good year if the following year is expected to be a challenging one, or delaying the recognition of expenses in a difficult year because performance is expected to improve in the near future.

The relationship between earnings smoothing and EQ is controversial. On the one hand, small variable earnings can be considered of high quality because they can be forecasted with a lower error than can high-variability earnings (Biddle & Hilary, 2006; Burgstahler et al., 2006; Gutiérrez & Rodríguez, 2019; Lang, Raedy, & Yetman, 2003; Schipper & Vincent, 2003). On the other hand, if managers recur to EM to smooth earnings, this manipulation would introduce noise in accounting information, thereby reducing EQ. Earnings smoothing is considered a manipulative technique to reduce natural earnings variability (VAR). Firms often attempt to control the fluctuations of reported earnings and steer them to levels that they consider desirable. In this view, smoother earnings imply lower EQ (Dechow & Skinner, 2000; Zeghal, Chtourou, & Fourati, 2012). For example, artificially smoothed earnings are not representative of the reporting entity's business model and its economic environment as in this case smoothing is an attempt to mask a firm's "true" performance. In these circumstances, smoothness is negatively associated with EQ and it is considered to be a consequence of EM, i.e., deliberated smoothing by managers (Leuz et al., 2003).

Under an alternative view, smoothness should be considered positively associated with EQ. This alternative point of view starts with the observation that the objective of accounting is to determine earnings (operating cash flows plus accounting accruals) and that the purpose of accruals is to smooth cash flows by filtering out some of their volatility. Similarly to persistence and predictability, a smoother earnings stream is less volatile and makes better forecasting possible. Some smoothing must therefore be desirable since management uses its private information to decide about the amount of bias so that smoothing incorporates private information about future cash flows into current earnings ("forward" smoothing). In this regard, prior studies provided evidence that practitioners (Graham, Harvey, & Rajgopal, 2005) and investors (Rountree, Weston, & Allayannis, 2008) view smoothness as a desirable attribute of earnings. A recent study (Baik, Choi, & Farber, 2019) found that high ability of managers in incorporating more forward-looking information about cash flows into current earnings through smoothing enhances earnings informativeness.

VAR is measured as the standard deviation (σ) of earnings (Hodder, Hopkins, & Wahlen, 2006).

$$\text{VAR}_i = \sigma\left(X_{i,t}\right)$$

where $X_{i,t}$ is firm i's earnings in year t.

Higher (lower) values represent higher (lower) levels of VAR, which are interpreted as lower (higher) EQ.

Earnings smoothing is usually measured as the ratio of VAR to cash flow variability (standard deviation of cash flows).

$$\text{ESM}_i = \frac{\sigma\left(X_{i,t}\right)}{\sigma\left(\text{CFO}_{i,t}\right)}$$

where $X_{i,t}$ is firm i's earnings in year t and $\text{CFO}_{i,t}$ is the cash flow from operations in year t.

Lower (higher) values indicate higher (lower) variability in cash flows than in earnings and, therefore, a higher (lower) level of artificial earnings smoothing.

Table 2.1 lists the earnings measures as commonly used proxies for (or indicators of) EQ and the most common specifications of the variables. For each measure, we summarize the definition and the construction.

Table 2.1 Summary of EQ proxies

Earnings attributes	*Definition*	*Calculation*
Earnings persistence	Stability of earnings (degree to which unexpected earnings from one period persist in future periods)	Slope coefficient from autoregressive models of earnings $X_{i,t} = \beta_0 + \beta_{1,i} X_{i,t-1} + \varepsilon_{i,t}$ (2.1) $\text{PER}_i = -\beta_1$
Earnings predictability	Ability of earnings to be predicted	Square root of the estimation error of Eq. (2.1) $\text{PRED}_i = \sqrt{\sigma^2 \varepsilon_{i,t}}$
Earnings variability	Real volatility of earnings	Standard deviation of earnings $\text{VAR}_i = \sigma(X_{1,t})$
Earnings smoothing	Intentional reduction in earnings variability	Standard deviation of earnings divided by the standard deviation of cash flows $\text{ESM}_i = \frac{\sigma(X_{i,t})}{\sigma(\text{CFO}_{i,t})}$

2.3.4 *Value Relevance*

The most common market-based measure of EQ is value relevance. In the extant literature, an accounting amount is defined as value relevant if it has a predicted association with equity market values. Earnings that are high in quality generally should also be more value relevant (Ferrer et al., 2016). In much of the accounting research into financial reporting quality, EQ is measured by its value relevance to investors in relation to equity valuation (Cheng, Hsieh, & Yip, 2007; Lang et al., 2003; Lang, Raedy, & Wilson, 2006; Leuz et al., 2003) or it is generally described as the ability of earnings to explain variation in stock return (Francis et al., 2004). If the relation between earnings and stock return is stronger, investors can rely more on the earnings figures to evaluate the company. Therefore, a higher relation between stock changes and earnings would indicate more reliable earnings.

It can be argued that value relevance is a measure for both reliability and relevance. The primary purpose of conducting tests of value relevance is to extend our knowledge regarding the relevance and reliability of accounting amounts as reflected in equity values. An accounting amount will be value relevant (i.e., have a predicted significant relation with share prices) only if the amount reflects relevant information for investors in valuing the firm and is measured enough reliably to be reflected in share prices (Barth, Li, & McClure, 2019). An accounting amount is relevant if it is capable of making a difference in the decisions made by users.[6] An accounting amount is reliable if it represents what it purports to represent. There are several dimensions of relevance and reliability. Dimensions of relevance include feedback value, predictive value, and timeliness. Dimension of reliability includes representational faithfulness, verifiability, and neutrality.

2.4 Timely Loss Recognition, Conservatism, and Accruals

The demand for reporting quality is based on the information asymmetry between management and stakeholders of the company (e.g., shareholders and lenders). Stakeholders require timely measures of performance for compensation purposes, debt agreements, and other contracts with the firm. Hence, timeliness of earnings is regarded as an important attribute of financial reporting quality (Ball & Shivakumar, 2005; Beekes, Pope, & Young, 2004). Timeliness is defined as the length of time taken to reflect information in earnings. In this perspective, timeliness of loss recognition is a summary indicator of the speed with which adverse economic events are reflected in both income statements and balance sheets.

The concept of timeliness is also related to conservatism.[7] Conservatism is a prudent reaction to uncertainty, reflecting in accounting the risk and uncertainty of a firm's performance (Mora & Walker, 2015). The use of timely loss recognition would result in recognizing losses

[6] Note also that the concepts of value relevance and decision relevance differ. In particular, accounting information can be value relevant but not decision relevant if it is superseded by more timely information.

[7] No authoritative definition of conservatism exists. As a result, different interpretations of conservatism have developed in the literature. Watts and Zimmerman (1986) provided the following definition: "Conservatism means that the accountant should report the lowest value among the possible alternative values for assets and the highest alternative value for liabilities. Revenues should be recognized later rather than sooner and expenses sooner than later". In his seminal paper, Basu (1997) makes an important contribution to the understanding of the conservatism concept. He defines conservatism as follows: "I interpret conservatism as capturing accountants' tendency to require a higher degree of verification for recognizing good news than bad news in financial statements. Under my interpretation of conservatism, earnings reflect bad news more quickly than good news".

quicker than possible profits, thus resulting in more prudent or conservative reporting. The accounting treatment of gains and losses is asymmetric when concerning the verification requirement. This difference is induced by the conservatism principle of accounting. Accounting research literature has distinguished two types of conservatism: conditional and unconditional. Conditional conservatism requires a higher degree of verification for recognizing good news than for bad news. This type of conservatism is expected to increase EQ because it helps to reduce the overinvestment problem, to constrain income-increasing accruals manipulation and to enhance debt-contracting efficiency (Beatty, Petacchi, & Zhang, 2012; Beatty, Weber, & Yu, 2008; Cano-Rodríguez & Nunez-Nickel, 2015; Wittenberg-Moerman, 2008; Zhang, 2008). The most common measures of conditional conservatism are based on the loss differential timeliness concept: Under conditional conservatism, the requirements for recognizing good news (gains) are stricter than those for recognizing bad news (losses), so losses are recorded more timely than gains. As the differential verifiability is required for the recognition of profits versus losses, conservative earnings reflect bad news more quickly than good news. Therefore, conservatism causes more timely recognition of losses than gains and improves quality of accounting information in the context of corporate governance and loan agreements. Asymmetric timely recognition of losses relative to gains is often labeled as conditional conservatism (ex-post conservatism or earnings conservatism). Conditional conservatism acts as an instrument of corporate governance in preventing management manipulations of reported earnings, and thus it is considered to be a desirable attribute of financial reporting (Alzoubi & Selamat, 2012; Beaver & Ryan, 2005; Mora & Walker, 2015; Richardson & Tinaikar, 2004). Anyway, conservatism implies the exercise of caution in the recognition and measurement of income and assets.

Unconditional conservatism (balance sheet conservatism or ex-ante conservatism) is the choice of a lower (higher) than expected value in the estimation of assets or revenue (liabilities or expenses) valuation under uncertainty (Ball & Shivakumar, 2005). Unconditional conservatism is associated with a lower EQ level and various empirical studies have demonstrated that it can provide more opportunities for earnings manipulation (Jackson & Liu, 2010; Ruch & Taylor, 2015) and lead to inefficient investments. Unconditional conservatism reflects the application of conservative accounting policies (e.g., expenditure of R&D and advertising) where conditional conservatism is event-driven. Under conservative accounting, firms build reserves and understate their reported earnings when investments in operating assets increase. In contrast, if investments decrease, built reserves could get released. Either way, changes in growth under conservative accounting affect EQ due to earnings becoming temporarily bloated or inflated. Ignoring these changes could consequently distort forecasts which simply fixate on earnings what is reported in the financial statements.

We interpret earnings that reflect losses on a more timely basis as being of higher quality. The principles of accrual accounting are used in financial reporting to provide a timely measure of performance. We discuss the role of accruals for the timely recognition of unrealized gains and losses. An exclusive focus on bottom-line income misses important information contained in accruals (the difference between accounting earnings and cash flow) about the quality of earnings. Earnings' increases that are accompanied by high accruals—suggesting low quality of earnings—are associated with poor future returns. Assessment of EQ requires sometimes the separations of earnings into cash from operation and accruals: The more the earnings are closed to cash from operation, the higher EQ. Accounting income is the main indicator of financial reporting and it consists of the cash flow generated by the operations of a firm and accruals adjustments on cash flow from operations based on expectations of cash flows. The difference between earnings and cash flow data is the accrual adjustments. Therefore, the ultimate question is whether accrual data contain information that improves valuation forecasts. Most of practitioners and academics agree that cash flows are more reliable than earnings. Unlike earnings that contain accruals, cash flows are not estimated. But considering the estimations involved in determining earnings and the opportunities that exist for companies to manage earnings, cash flows can be thought of as relatively reliable.

The primary function of accruals is to reduce the noise in transitory cash flows to produce earnings. Realized cash flows have timing and matching problems that cause them to be a "noisy" measure of firm performance. Accruals alter the timing of cash flows' recognition in earnings to mitigate the noise in cash flows. This results in a negative correlation between accruals and cash flow from operations. The other major function of accruals is the timely recognition of unrealized gains and losses. Accruals represent the difference between a firm's accounting earnings and its underlying cash flow. Large positive accruals indicate that earnings are much higher than cash flows. Earnings and cash flow can differ because accounting conventions with respect to the timing and magnitude of revenues and expenses (the so-called revenue recognition and matching principles) are not necessarily based on cash flows and outflows. Some revenues can be counted toward earnings in the current period, for example, even though they have not yet been received in cash. Similarly, certain expenses (such as depreciation) are deducted from revenues even though they entail non-cash outlays.

Regarding the role of accruals for the determination of EQ, they are used to give a better view of a company performance. The primary result of financial reporting is net income (or earnings) as a measure of performance, where earnings are the summary measure of firm performance produced under the accrual basis of accounting. Accounting accruals have recently gained attention as an important indicator related to EQ. The most widely used construct to measure EQ is through the discretionary accruals model that captures EM (discretionary accruals imply EM and lower quality of earnings). Accruals can introduce a transitory element in earnings that reduces the beneficial use of them for the evaluation of future performance. Based on the amount of accruals, we can define EQ as the degree of the closeness of a company's earnings to the amount of cash flow. As a result, accruals can affect the quality of earnings since the less the level of accruals, the more the quality of earnings. One common approach is to split accruals into "normal" and "abnormal" accruals, based on a forecast model for total accruals. Abnormal accruals are the difference between actual and expected accruals. Higher (absolute) abnormal accruals are commonly interpreted as meaning lower EQ, because the firm's accrual process is less predictable and abnormal accruals are likely to be discretionary, i.e., as the result of EM.

EQ can vary among companies as a function of accruals even in the absence of intentional earnings manipulation. Unlike cash flows, the determination of earnings requires estimations and judgments, and some companies need more forecasts and estimates than others. For example, companies in growing industries typically have high accruals, which raise a question about reliability because accruals are likely to contain estimation errors. Therefore, large accruals (of either sign) can indicate great underlying volatility in the company's operations and low quality of earnings (under our definition), even when the company is complying with

Generally Accepted Accounting Principles (GAAPs) and it does not act opportunistically.

If implemented properly, accrual accounting should result in earnings that reflect the underlying economic variation in the company's operations. Otherwise, accrual accounting opens the door to opportunistic short-run income smoothing that can lead to future restatements and write-downs. EQ can be improved when accruals smooth out value irrelevant changes in cash flows, but EQ is reduced when accruals are used to hide value relevant changes in cash flows. Distinguishing between these two types of accrual adjustments is critical to financial analysis.

The accrual adjustments enable earnings to be a better predictor of future cash flows than current ones. Accruals mirror the expectations of future cash flows of the firm's managers but GAAPs provide a variety of methods to calculate accruals based on managers' expectations of future cash flows.

In fact, the use of accruals introduces potential problems, since managers typically have some discretion over the accruals' recognition. This discretion can be used by management to signal their private information or to opportunistically manipulate earnings. Signaling is likely to develop the ability of earnings to measure firm performance since managers presumably have more information about their firm's cash generating ability. However, if managers use their discretion to opportunistically manipulate accruals, earnings become a less reliable measure of firm performance. The accrual process in those cases is not beneficial in predicting future cash flows and current cash flows could be preferred over current earnings when forming outlooks of future payoffs to stocks' holders.

An astute analyst cannot focus on earnings alone. One approach is to measure how closely cash flows track with changes in working capital. In this model, any change in working capital that cannot be explained by cash flows results in lower quality accruals. Because EQ informs investors about the recording of accounting earnings into cash flows, poor quality of earnings' reports increases information risk by weakening this relationship.

To assess EQ, the analyst must evaluate the company's cash flow statement and balance sheet in conjunction with the income statement. In this case, book values are written down under sufficiently adverse circumstances but not written up under favorable circumstances, with the latter being the conservative behavior. An important consequence of conservatism's asymmetric treatment of gains and losses is the persistent understatement of net asset values.

2.5 Different Methods to Measure Earnings Quality

A company cannot be assessed as having poor or high EQ by using only one method. Since operational definition of EQ is difficult, stakeholders should select more than one method for the assessment of EQ before any investment decision-making. In particular, EQ can be measured using 4 different criteria.

The Penman Index (operational cash flow to net profit ratio) measures the quality using conservatism principle (Penman & Zhang, 2002). Managers tend to announce the net earnings so that in successive years they show growth. In years with high net profit, the management worries that in incoming years the profit may go down and its performance would be under question. So managers tend to be conservative in calculating earnings and thus they transfer a portion of earnings to future. The transferred earnings are recognized in incoming years so that the profitability of the company is shown to be properly growing. This is done normally through transferring the non-operational revenues and costs to future. Since cash items can less be manipulated, this is done via non-operational accrued revenues and costs. In these circumstances, "operational cash flow to net profit ratio" is used to measure EQ. If the management using conservatism has been avoiding to identify some of net earnings, this ratio would increase and this increasing means the decrease of EQ. In other words, the more management is conservative the more this ratio and the less EQ would be.

Leuz Index (Leuz et al., 2003) focuses on profit changeability which is in turn is based on managers' tendency to smooth income. The degree with which the variability of reported earnings is reduced by using accruals can be measured using the following measure. EQ is measured by the variability of earnings (which is equal to the standard deviation of operating income) divided by the standard deviation of cash flow from operations, to control for differences in the variability of firms' economic performance. Operational earnings consist of cash flow and accrual items. Operational earnings can be manipulated while operational cash flow is less subjected to manipulation. With smoothing of income, standard deviation of operating income in several successive years will become less than operational cash flow standard deviation. So, the low number of the Leuz Index is indicative of low EQ.

Jones Model is used to estimate discretionary accruals. Jones (1991) used the discretionary accruals to measure earnings manipulation, where the changes in total accruals are due exclusively to changes in discretionary accruals, because non-discretionary accruals remain constant. The result of pulling discretionary accrual amounts from the total accrual amount is a metric that reflects accruals that are due to management's choices alone; in other words, there appears to be no business reason for these accruals. So, discretionary accruals are a proxy for EQ. The component of the accrual that is imposed by the accounting regulator in adjusting a firm's cash flows is the non-discretionary accruals. The accruals component that managers can choose within the flexibility of accounting regulations in adjusting a firm's cash flows is the discretionary accruals.

Earnings are composed of two components: total accruals and cash flows from operations. Total accruals are accounting adjustments to the firm's cash flows and can result from management discretion or from changes in a firm's economic environment. The main purpose of this accruals-based model is to separate total accruals in discretionary and non-discretionary accruals.

Hence, the starting point of the abovementioned model is obtained distinguishing "abnormal"[8] from "normal" accruals by directly modeling the accrual process. The normal accruals are meant to capture adjustments that reflect fundamental performance, while the abnormal accruals are meant to capture distortions induced by application of the accounting rules or EM (i.e., due to an imperfect measurement system). The general interpretation is that if the "normal" component of accruals is modeled properly, then the abnormal component represents a distortion that signifies a low quality.

Basically, non-discretionary accruals (i.e., normal accruals) are related to the normal performance of the company. The other portion of total accruals is discretionary accruals (i.e., abnormal accruals) which capture the distortions induced by the application of Accounting Standards or by intentional intervention of managers to manipulate earnings. A high level of discretionary accruals implies higher opportunity of EM and then lower EQ. Prior studies distinguish EM based on discretionary accruals. The earnings have two components, cash flow from operations and total

[8] We use "discretionary accruals" interchangeably with abnormal accruals, even though it is somewhat loaded term that seems more associated with an active choice rather than an outcome of the measurement system or error.

Table 2.2 EQ criteria

	Penman	*Leuz*	*Jones Model*	*Dichev and Dechow Model*
Criteria	EQ is measured by the ratio of cash flow from operation divided by the net income (profit)	EQ is measured by the variability of earnings (standard deviation of operating income) divided by the standard deviation of cash flow from operations	EQ is measured by the absolute value of discretionary accruals	EQ is measured by the standard deviation of residuals from firm-specific working capital regression based on current, regression model of changes in working capital regression based on past, present, and future operating cash flows
Relationship between the criteria and EQ	The smaller the ratio, the higher EQ	The smaller the ratio, the lower EQ	The smaller the value, the higher the quality of earnings	The smaller the standard deviation, the higher EQ

accruals. The total accruals are management's judgments and estimates about cash flows for making accounting earnings better reflecting a firm's underlying economic performance. Total accruals are the sum of discretionary accruals and non-discretionary accruals. Discretionary accruals often provide managers the opportunities to manipulate earnings due to the flexibility available within accounting systems. Discretionary accrual is subjected to managerial discretion while non-discretionary accruals are the expected level of accruals in the firm on condition that there is no manipulation of earnings.

From another perspective, Dechow and Dichev (2002) developed a measure of the accruals quality based on past, present, and future cash flows. According to the authors, accruals quality is measured through the working capital equation error, where a higher standard deviation of the residues means lower EQ. Dechow and Dichev Model (2002) expresses

EQ as the magnitude of estimation errors in accruals and provides empirical estimates of this measure based on the relation between accruals and cash flows. One role of accruals is to shift or adjust the recognition of cash flows over time so that the adjusted numbers (earnings) better measure firm performance. However, accruals require assumptions and estimates of future cash flows. The quality of accruals and earnings is decreasing in the magnitude of estimation error in accruals. In this approach, the remainder of working capital regression based on current, past, and future cash flows for a certain company shows the total estimation error of accruals (both unintentional and manipulated by management) and is used as a reverse criterion for EQ. Within the Model, the standard deviation of residuals is used as a company-level measure of accruals and EQ, in which a high match between accruals and cash flows is signified by a low standard deviation, implying both high-quality accruals and earnings (Table 2.2).

Since, there is not any consensus regarding the definition of EQ or its measurement techniques, we cannot classify a company in high or low EQ categories only based on one technique. In other words, if there is not any compatibility among the results of more than one method of EQ measurement, one cannot comment on EQ of that company. The indices do not confirm one another for every company. Therefore, investors and creditors have to consider more than one criterion in their assessments. In fact, shareholders cannot assert anything about the EQ of a company if the assessment based on one criterion results in low EQ and that based on another one shows a high quality.

Bibliography

Alzoubi, E. S., & Selamat, M. H. (2012). The effectiveness of corporate governance mechanisms on constraining earning management: Literature review and proposed framework. *International Journal of Global Business, 5*(1), 17–35.

Anctil, R. M., & Chamberlain, S. (2005). Determinants of the time series of earnings and implications for earnings quality. *Contemporary Accounting Research, 22*(3), 483–517.

Baik, B., Choi, S., & Farber, D. B. (2019, October 11). Managerial ability and income smoothing. *The Accounting Review*, in-press. Available at: https://doi.org/10.2308/accr-52600.

Ball, R., & Shivakumar, L. (2005). Earnings quality in UK private firms: Comparative loss recognition timeliness. *Journal of Accounting and Economics, 39*(1), 83–128.

Balsam, S., Krishnan, J., & Yang, J. S. (2003). Auditor industry specialization and earnings quality. *Auditing: A Journal of Practice & Theory, 22*(2), 71–97.

Barragato, C., & Markelevich, A. (2008). Earnings quality following corporate acquisitions. *Managerial Finance, 34*(5), 304–315.

Barth, M. E., Landsman, W. R., & Lang, M. H. (2008). International accounting standards and accounting quality. *Journal of Accounting Research, 46*(3), 467–498.

Barth, M. E., Li, K., & McClure, C. (2019, August 22). *Evolution in value relevance of accounting information* (Stanford University Graduate School of Business Research, Paper No. 17–24). Available at SSRN: https://ssrn.com/abstract=2933197.

Bartov, E., & Mohanram, P. (2004). Private information, earnings manipulations, and executive stock-option exercises. *The Accounting Review, 79*(4), 889–920.

Basu, S. (1997). The conservatism principle and the asymmetric timeliness of earnings. *Journal of Accounting and Economics, 24*(1), 3–37.

Beatty, A., Petacchi, R., & Zhang, H. (2012). Hedge commitments and agency costs of debt: Evidence from interest rate protection covenants and accounting conservatism. *Review of Accounting Studies, 17,* 700–738.

Beatty, A., Weber, J., & Yu, J. J. (2008). Conservatism and debt. *Journal of Accounting and Economics, 45*(2–3), 154–174.

Beaver, W. H., & Ryan, S. G. (2005). Conditional and unconditional conservatism: Concepts and modeling. *Review of Accounting Studies, 10*(2–3), 269–309.

Beekes, W., Pope, P. F., & Young, S. (2004). The link between earnings timeliness, earnings conservatism and board composition: Evidence from the UK. *Corporate Governance: An International Review, 12*(1), 47–59.

Biddle, G. C., & Hilary, G. (2006). Accounting quality and firm-level capital investment. *The Accounting Review, 81*(5), 963–982.

Bodie, Z., Kane, A., & Marcus, A. J. (2002). *Investments* (5th ed.). New York: McGraw-Hill.

Bricker, R., Previts, G., Robinson, T., & Young, S. (1995). Financial analyst assessment of company earnings quality. *Journal of Accounting, Auditing & Finance, 10*(3), 541–554.

Burgstahler, D. C., Hail, L., & Leuz, C. (2006). The importance of reporting incentives: Earnings management in European private and public firms. *The Accounting Review, 81*(5), 983–1016.

Cano-Rodríguez, M., & Nunez-Nickel, M. (2015). Aggregation bias in estimates of conditional conservatism: Theory and evidence. *Journal of Business Finance and Accounting, 42*(1–2), 51–78.

Chen, L. H., Folsom, D. M., Paek, W., & Sami, H. (2014). Accounting conservatism, earnings persistence, and pricing multiples on earnings. *Accounting Horizons, 28*(2), 233–260.

Cheng, A., Hsieh, S., & Yip, Y. (2007). Impact of accounting choices on firm valuation and earnings quality. *Review of Accounting and Finance, 6*(4), 419–441.

Clubb, C., & Wu, G. (2014). Earnings volatility and earnings prediction: Analysis and UK evidence. *Journal of Business Finance & Accounting, 41*(1–2), 53–72.

Cornell, B., & Landsman, W. R. (2003). Accounting valuation: Is earnings quality an issue? *Financial Analysts Journal, 59*(6), 20–28.

DeAngelo, L. (1986). Accounting numbers as market valuation substitutes: A study of management buyouts of public stockholders. *The Accounting Review, 61*(3), 400–420.

Dechow, P. M., & Dichev, I. D. (2002). The quality of accruals and earnings: The role of accrual estimation errors. *The Accounting Review, 77*(Suppl.), 35–59.

Dechow, P. M., Ge, W., & Schrand, C. (2010). Understanding earnings quality: A review of the proxies, their determinants and their consequences. *Journal of Accounting and Economics, 50*(2–3), 344–401.

Dechow, P. M., & Schrand, C. M. (2004). *Earnings quality.* Charlottesville, VA, USA: Research Foundation of CFA Institute.

Dechow, P. M., & Skinner, D. J. (2000). Earnings management: Reconciling the views of accounting academics. *Practitioners, and Regulators, Accounting Horizons, 14*(2), 235–250.

Dechow, P. M., Sloan, R. G., & Sweeney, A. P. (1995). Detecting earnings management. *The Accounting Review, 70*(2), 193–225.

Dichev, I. D., Graham, J. R., Harvey, C. R., & Rajgopal, S. (2013). Earnings quality: Evidence from the field. *Journal of Accounting and Economics, 56*(2–3), 1–33.

Dichev, I. D., & Tang, V. W. (2008). Matching and the changing properties of accounting earnings over the last 40 years. *The Accounting Review, 83*(6), 1425–1460.

Donnelly, R. (2002). Earnings persistence, losses and the estimation of earnings response coefficients. *Abacus, 38*(1), 121–133.

Doyle, J., Lundholm, R. J., & Soliman, M. T. (2003). The predictive value of expenses excluded from pro forma earnings. *Review of Accounting Studies, 8*, 145–174.

Ewert, R., & Wagenhofer, A. (2010). *Earnings quality metrics and what they measure* (Working Paper), University of Graz, Austria, full text available at: http://dx.doi.org/10.1561/1400000025.

Ferrer, C., Callao, S., Jarne, I., & Lainez, J. (2016). A structural equation model for analyzing the association between some attributes of earnings quality and value relevance. *Modeling and Simulation in Engineering, Economics and Management, 115*, 31–39.

Francis, J., LaFond, R., Olsson, P. M., & Schipper, K. (2003, April). Earnings quality and the pricing effects of earnings patterns. *SSRN Electronic Journal*, 1–52. http://dx.doi.org/10.2139/ssrn.414142.

Francis, J., LaFond, R., Olsson, P. M., & Schipper, K. (2004). Costs of equity and earnings attributes. *The Accounting Review, 79*(4), 967–1010.

Gaio, C. (2010). The relative importance of firm and country characteristics for earnings quality around the world. *European Accounting Review, 19*(4), 693–738.

Graham, J. R., Harvey, C., & Rajgopal, S. (2005). The economic implications of corporate financial reporting. *Journal of Accounting and Economics, 40*(1–3), 3–73.

Gutiérrez, A. L., & Rodríguez, M. C. (2019). A review on the multidimensional analysis of earnings quality. *Spanish Accounting Review, 22*(1), 41–60.

Hirst, D. E., Hopkins, P. E., & Wahlen, J. M. (2004). Fair values, income measurement, and bank analysts' risk and valuation judgments. *The Accounting Review, 79*(2), 453–472.

Hodder, L. D., Hopkins, P. E., & Wahlen, J. M. (2006). Risk-relevance of fair-value income measures for commercial banks. *The Accounting Review, 81*(2), 337–375.

IASB. (2010). *Conceptual framework for financial reporting* (Conceptual framework).

Jackson, S. B., & Liu, X. (2010). The allowance for uncollectible accounts, conservatism, and earnings management. *Journal of Accounting Research, 48*(3), 565–601.

Jonas, G. J., & Blanchet, J. (2000). Assessing quality of financial reporting. *Accounting Horizons, 14*(3), 353–363.

Jones, J. (1991). Earnings management during import relief investigations. *Journal of Accounting Research, 29*(2), 193–228.

Khaled, E. A. (2005). Measuring the quality of earnings. *Managerial Auditing Journal, 20*(9), 1001–1015.

Kormendi, R., & Lipe, R. (1987). Earnings innovations, earnings persistence, and stock returns. *The Journal of Business, 60*(3), 323–345.

Kousenidis, D. V., Ladas, A. C., & Negakis, P. (2013). The effects of the European debt crisis on earnings quality. *International Review of Financial Analysis, 30*, 351–362.

Krishnan, G. V., & Zhang, J. (2019). Does mandatory adoption of IFRS enhance earnings quality? Evidence from closer to home. *The International Journal of Accounting, 54*(1), 1–42.

Lang, M., Raedy, J. S., & Wilson, W. (2006). Earnings management and cross listing: Are reconciled earnings comparable to US earnings? *Journal of Accounting and Economics, 42*(1–2), 255–283.

Lang, M., Raedy, J. S., & Yetman, M. H. (2003). How representative are firms that are cross-listed in the United States? An analysis of accounting quality. *Journal of Accounting Research, 41*(2), 363–386.

Leuz, C., & Wysocki, P. D. (2016). The economics of disclosure and financial reporting regulation: Evidence and suggestions for future research. *Journal of Accounting Research, 54*(2), 525–622.

Leuz, C., Nanda, D., & Wyscocki, P. D. (2003). Earnings management and investor protection: An international comparison. *Journal of Financial Economics, 69*(3), 505–527.

Lipe, R. C. (1990). The relation between stock returns and accounting earnings given alternative information. *The Accounting Review, 65*(1), 49–71.

McDaniel, L., Martin, R. D., & Maines, L. A. (2002). Evaluating financial reporting quality: The effects of financial expertise vs. financial literacy. *The Accounting Review, 77*(Suppl.), 139–167.

Mora, A., & Walker, M. (2015). The implications of research on accounting conservatism for accounting standard setting. *Accounting and Business Research, 45*(5), 620–650.

Penman, S. H., & Zhang, X.-J. (2002). Accounting conservatism, the quality of earnings, and stock returns. *The Accounting Review, 77*(2), 237–264.

Perotti, P., & Wagenhofer, A. (2014). Earnings quality measures and excess returns. *Journal of Business Finance & Accounting, 41*(5), 545–571.

Peterson, K., Schmardebeck, R., & Wilks, T. J. (2015). The earnings quality and information processing effects of accounting consistency. *The Accounting Review, 90*(6), 2483–2514.

Revsine, L., Collins, D. W., & Johnson, W. B. (2002). *Financial reporting & analysis.* Upper Saddle River, NJ: Prentice Hall.

Richardson, G., & Tinaikar, S. (2004). Accounting based valuation models: What have we learned? *Accounting & Finance, 44*(2), 223–255.

Richardson, S. A. (2003). Earnings quality and short sellers. *Accounting Horizons, 17*(s-1), 49–61.

Richardson, S. A., Sloan, R. G., Soliman, M. T., & Tuna, A. I. (2005). Accrual reliability, earnings persistence and stock prices. *Journal of Accounting and Economics, 39*(3), 437–485.

Rountree, B., Weston, J. P., & Allayannis, G. (2008). Do investors value smooth performance? *Journal of Financial Economics, 90*(3), 237–251.

Ruch, G. W., & Taylor, G. (2015, February). Accounting conservatism: A review of the literature. *Journal of Accounting Literature, 34*, 17–38.

Schipper, K. (2003). Principles-based accounting standards. *Accounting Horizons, 17*(1), 61–72.

Schipper, K., & Vincent, L. (2003). Earnings quality. *Accounting Horizons, 17* (s-1), 97–110.

Sloan, R. (1996). Do stock prices fully reflect information in accruals and cash flows about future earnings? *The Accounting Review, 71*(3), 289–315.

Teets, R. W. (2002). Quality of earnings: An introduction to the issues in accounting education [Special issue]. *Issues in Accounting Education, 17*(4), 335–360.

Van der Meulen, S., Gaeremynck, A., & Willekens, M. (2007). Attribute differences between U.S. GAAP and IFRS earnings: An explanatory study. *The International Journal of Accounting, 42*(2), 123–142.

Watts, R. L., & Zimmerman, J. L. (1986). *Positive accounting theory*. Englewood Cliffs: Prentice Hall.

Wittenberg-Moerman, R. (2008). The role of information asymmetry and financial reporting quality in debt trading. *Journal of Accounting and Economics, 46*(2–3), 240–260.

Zeghal, D., Chtourou, S. M., & Fourati, Y. M. (2012). The effect of mandatory adoption of IFRS on earnings quality: Evidence from the European Union. *Journal of International Accounting Research, 11*(2), 1–25.

Zhang, J. (2008). The contracting benefits of accounting conservatism to lenders and borrowers. *Journal of Accounting and Economics, 45*(1), 27–54.

CHAPTER 3

Earnings Quality and Earnings Management

Abstract Earnings management (EM) and earnings quality (EQ) can be considered two related challenging issues in financial reporting as EM is an aspect influencing EQ. Managers can make discretionary accounting choices that are regarded as a practice of either efficient communication of private information or distorting disclosure. When income smoothing is used to communicate private information and expectations, it can improve the informativeness of a firm's current and future performance. On the contrary, the intentional manipulation of earnings made by managers, within the limits allowed by the Accounting Standards, may distort the usefulness of financial reporting to users. In this circumstance, EM looks like a practice that could lead to lower quality of earnings if it identifies with the result of management's opportunistic use of accruals with the intent to mislead users.

Keywords Earnings quality (EQ) · Earnings management (EM) · Accrual accounting · Earnings smoothing · Accounting conservatism

3.1 Introduction

In the last decade, the role of reported earnings in the market place has notably increased. If a company's earnings per share miss analysts' forecast by only one cent, a company's stock price can fall several points.

E. Menicucci, *Earnings Quality*,
https://doi.org/10.1007/978-3-030-36798-5_3

News that a firm has fallen short of earnings expectations can immediately send its stock price plunging. On the other hand, firms that beat expectations are handsomely rewarded by investors. Analysts, managers, and investors all devote a great attention to firms' reported earnings. Because of potential adverse market reactions, companies often take unusual actions to avoid reporting losses. The increased market reactions to missed earnings forecasts and the nearly constant need of corporations for external financing, incentive companies to manage earnings.

Prior studies (e.g., Dechow, Sloan, & Sweeney, 1995) underlined that an important motivation for earnings' manipulation is the desire to attract external financing at low cost. The focus on earnings is so intense that it has been suggested that the market fixates on firms' bottom-line income, excluding other indicators of operating performance. Such a single-minded attention fails to recognize that reported net income is the result of an extended accounting process with considerable room for managerial discretion at every step. The risks of focusing exclusively on bottom-line earnings have vividly intensified the attention on accounting income as managers have an incentive to be aggressive in applying accounting rules so as not to disappoint investors and analysts. For many years, it has been believed that a firm should attempt to reduce the volatility of its earnings stream in order to maximize share price. Because a highly volatile earnings pattern indicates risk, therefore the stock should lose value compared to others with more stable earnings patterns.

The pressure to meet expectations is particularly intense and it may be the primary catalyst in leading managers to engage in EM practices that result in questionable or fraudulent revenue recognition practices. Paradoxically, it is often the companies themselves that feed this pressure to meet the market's earnings expectations. It is common practice for companies to provide earnings' estimates to analysts and investors and management is often faced with the task of ensuring their targeted estimates.

Moreover, managers are keenly interested in maintaining growth in earnings and in smoothing them toward a long-term sustainable trend because their compensations are frequently tied to their firms' profits. Consequently, managers could have personal reasons to manage earnings with the aim to achieve a smooth and growing earnings stream. Sometimes, EM aims at meeting the bonus plan's requirements and at maximizing the executive's earnings-based bonus. When earnings are below the minimum level required to earn a bonus, then they are managed upward so that the minimum is achieved and a bonus is earned. Conversely, when earnings are above the maximum level at which no additional bonus is paid, then earnings are managed downward. The extra earnings that will not generate extra bonus in the current period are saved to be used to earn a bonus in a future period. When earnings are between the minimum and the maximum levels, then earnings are managed upward in order to increase the bonus earned in the current period. The Securities and Exchange Commission (SEC) cites hundreds of cases in which managers have used accounting maneuvers to inflate their firms' profits and, in this regard, there are a lot of examples of high-profile firms that have inflated earnings for extended periods.

A large body of studies has been developed within the EM stream of research and interest in this subject is yet high. Therefore, it is useful to get a better understanding of EM, discussing the extent to which it can be defined, measured, and related to EQ.

3.2 Earnings Management: Literature Review

Over the last few decades, several academic and business authors concluded that sometimes companies try to smooth or manage their reported earnings. EM receives a lot of attention in the academic press; moreover, regulators and practitioners believe that it is both pervasive and problematic. EM can be achieved through several means, e.g., using the discretion allowed under Accounting Standards, by changing firm's depreciation policy including depreciation methods and estimates, adjusting the estimate of the provisions for bad debts, changing the useful life and/or residual value of fixed assets through assets revaluations, classifying gains and losses as extraordinary items, not recognizing goodwill impairment or not recognizing goodwill amortization and/or write-offs.

The extant literature on EM suggests that it exists due to the important roles and functions played by the reported earnings. Managers may be inclined to manage earnings due to the existence of the firm's explicit and implicit contracts, the firm's relation with capital markets, the need for external financing, the political and regulatory environment or several other specific circumstances. For example, earnings numbers are normally included in management compensation and bonus contracts, debt covenants, management buyouts, proxy contests, valuation of initial public offering (IPOs), labor union negotiations, and lobbying on Accounting Standards and regulations.

There are numerous situations or incentives that may motivate management to become involved in EM. Researchers provided evidence that managers have strong incentives to manage earnings in order to maximize their bonus and compensations (Cheng, Warfield, & Ye, 2011; Indjejikian, 2014; Shuto, 2007; Teshima & Shuto, 2008), to avoid violation of debt covenants or to decrease the cost of debt (Carmo, Moreira, & Miranda, 2016; Ge & Kim, 2014; Jaggi & Lee, 2002; Shen & Huang, 2013), to circumvent industry and other regulations, to meet the earnings forecasts and targets issued by management or analysts (Dutta & Gigler, 2002) and to maximize the proceeds of IPOs (Alhadab, Clacher, & Keasey, 2015; Ball & Shivakumar, 2008; Chiraz & Anis, 2013; Gao, Cong, & Evans, 2015; Nagata, 2013).

3.3 Earnings Management: Definitions

Among research topics in accounting and finance, none is perhaps more challenging than EM as it explicitly involves potential wrongdoing, mischief, conflict, cloak and dagger and a sense of mystery. Auditors, regulators, investors, and researchers seek to find these wrongdoers and to solve the mystery, which might turn out to involve fraud.

EM must be defined before its discussion. Academics have no consensus on what EM is and there have been some attempts to define it. The lack of consensus on the definition of EM implies differing interpretations of empirical evidence in studies that seek to detect EM or to provide evidence of EM incentives. In this regard, it is useful to compare the following definitions.

Schipper (1989) defined EM as: "disclosure management in the sense of a purposeful intervention in the external financial reporting process, with the extent of obtaining some private gain, as opposed to merely facilitating the neutral operation of the process".

Similarly, for Healy and Wahlen (1999), EM occurs when managers use their judgment to change financial reporting either to mislead stakeholders about the true performance of the firm or to influence contractual outcomes that depend on the information presented in the financial statements.

Within these definitions, EM could occur in any part of the external disclosure process and could take a number of forms. EM is approached from an informational perspective, under which earnings are one of many signals that may be used to make certain decisions and judgments. This definition also allows EM to occur via timing real investment and financial decisions. If the timing issue delays or accelerates a discretionary expenditure for a very short period of time around the firm's fiscal year, timing real decisions can be considered a means of managing earnings. In line with this definition, a critical issue arises if readers interpret any real decisions—including those implying that managers decline profitable opportunities—as EM. It is unlikely to call EM a deviation from rational investment behavior as EM is a financial reporting phenomenon.

Hence, we define EM as a deliberate involvement of management in the financial reporting process—within the constraints of Generally Accepted Accounting Principles (GAAPs)—to generate a desired amount of reported earnings (Giroux, 2003).[1] This managerial behavior entails the disclosure of unreliable financial information to influence stakeholders' decision-making and then to achieve benefits only for the firm's managers. Consequently, EM is expected to be inversely related to EQ because manipulated earnings worsen decision-making process leading to investment inefficiencies (Biddle & Hilary, 2006).[2]

Healy and Wahlen (1999) instead take the perspective of the Standard Setters for financial reporting and the view that Accounting Standards add value when they enable financial statements to effectively portray differences in firm's economic positions and performance in a timely and credible manner. They focused on how much judgment managers exercise in financial reporting, according to the following definition of EM: "Earnings management occurs when managers use judgment in financial reporting and in structuring transactions to alter financial reports to either mislead some stakeholders about the underlying economic performance of the company or to influence contractual outcomes that depend on reported accounting numbers". According to this definition, EM has been defined as an attempt by the managers to mislead some stakeholders about the economic performance of the company or to influence contractual outcomes that may affect their compensation. Healy and

[1] This definition relates to artificial EM which includes both changes in accounting methods and classificatory choices.

[2] Accounting researchers distinguish between accounting-based EM and real EM. The accounting-based EM regards how managers manipulate reported accounting numbers to gain a private benefit. Real EM consists of manipulating the earnings through real investment decisions (made by managers) that are not respectful of accounting (e.g., reducing capital expenditures or discretionary expenses).

Wahlen (1999) assigned a negative value to EM, i.e., misleading behavior. Their definition points out that managers can use many ways to exercise judgment and that they do this to mislead stakeholders about the underlying economic performance of the firm. A common factor is that some degree of judgment and/or estimation is usually necessary in the application of Accounting Principles but the degree of judgment varies according to how measurable, predictable, and common a certain transaction or situation may be. In doing so, management can apply its policy for reserves and interpretation of the underlying assumptions in a manner that can be characterized as relatively "conservative" or "aggressive" in nature.

Decisions about using accounting judgment to make financial reports more informative for users do not fall within this EM's definition that moves away from the information perspective. In fact, the only form of EM that has a clear definition is maybe the most extreme form of it, i.e., financial fraud. In this case, the managerial intent is clear and it results in an equally clear definition of EM: "the intentional, deliberate, misstatement or omission of material facts, or accounting data, which is deceptive and, when considered with all the information made available, would cause the reader to change or alter his or her judgment or decision" (Dechow & Skinner, 2000).

The above definitions allow EM to occur for the purposes of hiding deteriorating performance, but the word "mislead" in the Healy and Wahlen (1999) definition appears to preclude the possibility that EM can occur for the purposes of enhancing the signal in reported earnings. According to this definition, EM shares much fraud that we can define as one or more intentional acts designed to deceive other persons and cause them financial loss. Anyway, it's difficult to distinguish whether managers' exercise of discretion is intended to mislead or to inform, and in this regard the typical conclusion of existing studies is that contractual incentives result in opportunistic EM.

In line with the Healy and Wahlen's (1999) managed earnings are of lower quality than unmanaged earnings as the greater the gap of reported earnings from what it should, the lower the quality of earnings. According to this description, EM leads to a distortion of the accounting numbers so that it decreases EQ as posited in most previous papers. Consistently, previous studies on EQ (Barth, Landsman, & Lang, 2008; Van Tendeloo & Vanstraelen, 2005) stated that when EM is on the rise, the quality of financial reporting is on the decline and they used the term "earnings quality" related to EM. Thus, any changes in the extent of managerial discretion may also change the amount of EM. According to the above definitions, it is clear that EM becomes possible due to the discretion given to managers when preparing financial reports. However, discretion is limited within the boundaries allowed by a particular set of Accounting Standards.

Although widely accepted, these definitions are difficult to be operationalized directly using attributes of reported accounting numbers since they center on managerial intent, which is unobservable. All the definitions deal with actions that managers undertake within the context of financial reporting, including the structuring of transactions so that a desired accounting treatment is applied (e.g., pooling, operating leases).

There are two perspectives on EM: (1) the information perspective under which managerial discretion is a means for managers to reveal their private expectations about the firm's future cash flow to investors (Kanagaretnam, Lim, & Lobo, 2014) and (2) the opportunistic perspective holds that managers seek to mislead investors. The informative perspective indicates that EQ is improved when managers report less noisy earnings by taking reporting actions that reveal accurate and precise information about firm's real performance. In this case, EM may be beneficial because it improves the information value of earnings by conveying private information to the stockholders and the public. On the contrary, from the opportunistic perspective, EM is regarded as a strategy used by management of a company to deliberately manipulate the company's earnings so that the earnings figures match a predetermined target. As a strategy, EM involves the planning and the execution of certain activities that manipulate and smooth income, achieve high EQ and influence the company's stock price. EQ decreases if managers behave opportunistically and interfere intentionally in the earnings reporting process by altering the firm economic performance to mislead outsiders and/or increase their own welfare at expense of investors. In other words, EM consists in manipulating the earnings to achieve a predetermined target set by the management. Abusive EM and fraudulent practices begin by engaging in EM's schemes (designed primarily to "smooth" earnings) to meet internally imposed earnings' forecasts and analysts' expectations. Even if EM does not explicitly violate accounting rules, it is an ethically questionable practice.

However, it is also true that managers have incentives to manipulate earnings (Ali & Zhang, 2015; Graham, Harvey, & Rajgopal, 2005; Matsumoto, 2002) and the quality of earnings decreases when incentives for EM are high. In this circumstance, EM looks like a practice that could lead to lower quality of earnings if it identifies with the result of management's opportunistic use of accruals with the intent to mislead users. Generally Accepted Accounting Principles offer some flexibility in preparing the financial statements and give to managers some freedom in selecting accounting policies and alternatives. EM uses the flexibility in financial reporting to alter the financial results of the firm. In this regard, we can define EM as a gray area where the accounting is perverted through practices by which reported earnings reflect the desires of management rather than the underlying financial performance of the company.

3.4 Earnings Management and Accrual Accounting

Understanding EM is one of the central questions in accounting. We examine how managers exercise judgment in financial reporting through accrual accounting[3] to report earnings that best measure firm performance. Accruals' shift or adjusted recognition of cash flows over time is intended to make financial reports more informative about the performance of the firms (Dechow, 1994; Dechow, Kothari, & Watts, 1998).[4] However, the professional literature and the financial press have raised questions on whether the effect of accruals is either to increase EQ and make financial reports more informative or to enhance EM. The crucial issue seems to be how managers use accruals to reach earnings' high quality.

Research has shown that the accrual accounting process results in earnings that are smoother than underlying cash flows, since accruals tend to be negatively related to cash flows. As managers inflate earnings above

[3] Accrual accounting is an accounting method that measures the performance and position of a company by recognizing economic events regardless of when transactions occur. The general idea is that economic events are recognized by matching revenues to expenses (the matching principle) at the time in which the transaction occurs rather than when payment is made or received.

[4] The term "accrual" is used here in a general sense and includes both accrual accounts (for which recognition in the income statement precedes cash receipts or disbursements) and deferral accounts (for which cash receipts or disbursements precede recognition in the income statement). One can also view accrual accounting from a "balance sheet" perspective, in the sense that accrual accounting involves the recognition of an entity's rights and obligations as they occur.

cash flows, accrual rises. High accruals may reflect, for example, increases in accounts receivable (as managers record sales prematurely) or decreases in current liabilities (as managers understate liabilities such as warranty expenses). Since investors fixate on reported bottom-line income, they are temporarily fooled. This circumstance has extensive consequences. It suggests, for instance, that it may be necessary to limit managers' discretion with respect to accounting, since in this condition investors apparently cannot untangle the valuation effect of reported earnings in a timely manner.

As the implementation of GAAPs requires management to make adjustments and estimates, managers could use their discretion over accounting accruals and accounting choices, presumably for a private purpose. However, GAAPs require management to make judgments and estimates in order to provide periodical financial reports. The critical issue is to distinguish regular accrual accounting from EM as certain forms of EM (such as income smoothing) often seem to be appropriate accounting choices.

The question is: When does the use of accruals hamper the informativeness and the usefulness of the accounting process? The answer is related to the different types of accruals. Accruals may be generated by the normal activities of the company (normal or non-discretionary accruals) or by managers' earnings manipulation (abnormal or discretionary accruals[5]). Earnings can be manipulated through incomes or expenditures whose cash flow counterpart is recognized in subsequent periods. The temporal matching of incomes or expenditures in accounting is recognized using accruals. The component of the accrual that is imposed by the accounting regulator in adjusting a firm's cash flows is the non-discretionary accruals. The accruals component that managers can choose within the flexibility of accounting regulations in adjusting a firm's cash flow is the discretionary accruals.

The earnings have two components, cash flow from operations and total accruals. The total accruals are management's judgments and estimates of cash flows for making accounting earnings better reflecting a firm's underlying economic performance. Hence, a different and significant area of research distinguishes "abnormal" from "normal" accruals

[5] We use "discretionary accruals" interchangeably with abnormal accruals, even though it is somewhat loaded term that seems more associated with an active choice rather than an outcome of the measurement system or error.

by directly modeling the accrual process. Specifically, many authors have used abnormal or unexpected accruals to measure EQ although actually some of them confuse EQ and EM because the mentioned accrual process is a measure of EM. The normal accruals are intended to capture adjustments that reflect fundamental performance, while the abnormal accruals are intended to capture distortions induced by the application of accounting rules or EM (i.e., due to an imperfect measurement system). These measures attempt to directly find problems with the accounting measurement system and consequently are particularly relevant to accounting researchers. The general interpretation is that if the "normal" component of accruals is modeled properly, then the abnormal component represents a distortion that undermines EQ.

Under accrual accounting, current experience is used to make accounting estimates for future periods and these estimates feed back into current-period earnings. Thus, the positive effect of real performance on earnings during booming economies is affected by the effects of optimistic forecasts concerning continued growth and investment opportunities. As the economy slows down, however, managers find increasingly difficult to meet the high earnings occurred during the boom times. Downturns mean fewer sales, more bad debts, and more obsolete inventory. The real fall in sales and earnings is exacerbated by the reversals of optimistic prior-period accruals. Hence, some managers use aggressive accounting—or even fraud—to avoid to report a decline in earnings.

3.5 Earnings Management and Earnings Smoothing

EM is often defined as income smoothing, which has been examined by numerous studies in the past (Dechow & Skinner, 2000). Income smoothing has long been discussed as a type of management accounting behavior or a management tactic. According to prior literature, earnings smoothing is a special case of EM by which managers selectively smooth out inter-temporal volatility in reported earnings with the scope of disclosing a stable earnings stream according to a framework of GAAPs (Beidleman, 1973; Goel & Thakor, 2003; Imhoff, 1981; Shaw, 2003; Ronen & Yaari, 2008).

In other words, income smoothing is a form of EM, and it is generally defined as the managers' intentional attempts to reduce abnormal fluctuations (equalization of income to a certain level in each period) in reported earnings over time by using special tools in accountancy (Gutiérrez & Rodríguez, 2019). With this aim, managers can take actions to increase earnings when they are relatively low and to decrease them when they are relatively high.[6] In most cases, EM is used to increase income in the current year at the expense of income in future years or, conversely, to decrease current earnings in order to increase income in the future.

Based on this technique of earnings manipulation, managers are tricky enough to restate their accounting earnings through moving income from good year to bad year or moving expense from bad year to good year in the short period. More specifically, management reduces income in periods when business performance is favorable and earnings are comparatively high and, by contrast, contrives income to create earnings in periods when business performance is unfavorable and income is comparatively low. Hence, smoothing moderates year-to-year fluctuations in income by shifting earnings from peak years to less successful ones, making earnings fluctuations less volatile. In other words, income smoothing is practiced in accounting to reduce the variability of the accounting results and sometimes it interferes with a firm's capacity to recognize bad economic news (i.e., economic losses).

However, management of some companies deliberately manipulates items of financial statements in order to stabilize profitability. Hence, managers can opportunistically smooth earnings using EM practices. From this point of view, earnings smoothing can be considered as a manipulation practice that introduces noise into accounting information, thereby reducing EQ. Managers might hide or delay variations in fundamental performance, at the expense of the usefulness of earnings (Gutiérrez & Rodríguez, 2019). Provided that other conditions are identical, income smoothing behavior consists in managing reported figures either to increase earnings when management believes its initially planned term-end settlement targets cannot be achieved or to decrease earnings when achievement of higher earnings than planned is certain may be implemented during a given fiscal period. In this regard, within statutory Accounting Standards, the aim of income smoothing is to decrease the variability of the accounting results (Leuz, Nanda, & Wyscocki, 2003) by the utilization of accounting discretion.

[6]The latter is an important characteristic of income smoothing since the managers' actions are not always to exaggerate earnings.

It is interesting for managers to reduce the investors' uncertainties or "risk measures" concerning the economic and financial situation of the entities they manage. We can separate two components of investor's uncertainty: fundamental economic uncertainty and information asymmetry between managers and investors due to reporting noise (Beyer, Guttman, & Marinovic, 2019). One type of fundamental uncertainty of "risk measure" is the variation or dispersion of earnings over time, which can be reduced via smoothing techniques. In this circumstances, lower firm risk—as perceived by investors—is one of the most popular motivations for income smoothing. Smoothed income enables a firm to avoid discounting in the capital market owing to business performance fluctuation and simultaneously brings about desirable consequences with respect to institutional contracts that the firm has stipulated with stakeholders (financial covenants, delisting requirements, management compensation contracts, etc.…). The idea that managers do prefer smoothed earnings is widely extended among practitioners and academics alike. If the assumption of market efficiency is dropped, smoothing can also be used by managers to mislead market participants about the profitability or risk situation of the firm in order to lower the cost of capital and to extract private benefits from the firm. Hence, management can set the smoothness of earnings to maximize its own utility. Besides, managers smooth earnings for two main reasons: First, they are assumed to improve business economic performance during the period and second, consistently positive earnings may raise the expectations of cash flows to investors, thereby increasing share prices (Francis, LaFond, Olsson, & Schipper, 2004). There are some motivations for the phenomenon of income smoothing, including the following:

- withhold private information in capital markets since managers enjoy a significant information advantage, relative to the market (managers' information at the disclosure date explains 50% of the variation in earnings) (Bertomeu, Ma, & Marinovic, 2016);
- evaluation of manager's performance: Managers might increase performance by income smoothing;
- stability of share-market value: Companies engage in smoothing because the income variability leading to fluctuation in share prices will discourage investors to buy shares;
- tax motivations: By income smoothing, a company might pay less taxes and reduce political costs;

- increasing shareholders' and managers' welfare;
- facilitating the capability of predicting income and enhancing the reliability of financial forecasts;
- reducing the perceived riskiness of the company by strategically withholding bad news (Bertomeu et al., 2016);
- meeting debt covenants;
- enhancing firm value.

From the information perspective, income smoothing can be defined as a deliberate attempt by management to signal information to financial users. In this perspective, income smoothing, as a discretionary attribute of earnings, conveys information. In efficient capital markets, rational investors cannot be misled by smooth earnings, since returns and cash flows are observable. When the signal is verifiable and management has private information about future earnings' realizations, smoothing is a vehicle to publicly disclose this information. Thus, in this case smoothness can only fulfill a signaling role. If the signal is unverifiable, smoothing is overlooked by market participants as "cheap talk". Although there is evidence that income smoothing takes place, its effect on earnings informativeness is largely unknown.

The literature hypothesizes two opposite effects of income smoothing on earnings informativeness (i.e., the amount of information about future earnings or cash flows included in current-period stock return). One viewpoint is that income smoothing results in altered information and thus in less informative stock process. On the other hand, income smoothing through efficient communication of private information about the firm's future expectations can lead to more informative stock prices.

Smoothing involves natural and intentional smoothing. Natural smoothing comprises technical automatisms of the accrual process without manipulation by management; it is the result from an income-generating process that produces a smooth stream of income. This type of smoothing is not EM since there is no manipulation. Intentional smoothing can either be a real smoothing or an artificial smoothing. The type of intentional income smoothing, therefore, depends on managerial intent. Smoothing may occur through the accounting processes of recognition, measurement, and disclosure, as well as intentionally. Hence, intentional smoothing can occur either by timing real business decisions (real smoothing) or by choosing accounting methods that allocate earnings over time in the desired manner (artificial smoothing). In both cases, executives act intentionally to smooth results. A real smoothing involves managers' change of the economic (revenue generating) events, such as the sale or purchase of fixed assets, which also affect cash flow. Real smoothing involves decisions that affect cash flows and dissipate firm value. Examples include the change of the investments' timing and the provision of promotional discounts or vendor financing to risky customers to pump up sales toward the end of the quarter.

Conversely, an artificial smoothing is the result of managers' change of accounting entries' timing. Common definitions view artificial income smoothing as the process of manipulating the time-series of earnings through the accrual process to make the reported income stream less variable although this process does not increase or decrease equity in the long run. Therefore, artificial income smoothing can be characterized as a form of EM. Theoretically, the more a firm employs income smoothing (i.e., uses accruals to reduce the variability of profits) the less there is possibility for the timely acknowledgment of future economic losses (i.e., bad economic news). Artificially smoothing implies the use of accruals, which does not affect cash flow and is not based on economic events; rather, it is similar to a postponement or anticipation of revenues and expenditures. This kind of smoothing is achieved primarily by using the reporting flexibility provided by GAAPs.

There are two conflicting views on smooth earnings. One view reflects the idea that managers artificially smooth out relevant fluctuations. Based on this view, earnings smoothness indicates poor quality of earnings which supports the hypothesis that management responds of a negative (positive) cash flow stream by increasing (decreasing) accruals. On the other side, managers follow real smoothing which involves decisions that affect cash flows and dissipate firm value. According to this point of view, management can achieve more useful earnings. In contrast with artificial smoothing, real smoothing indicates high quality of earnings (Francis, Olsson, & Schipper, 2008).

We fully share the point of view expressed by Gassen, Fülbier, and Sellhorn (2006), who contended that income smoothing interferes with the accounting accruals of firms by reducing the ability of accounting to reflect the economic reality of a business and by increasing information asymmetry in the capital market. Income smoothing also interferes with the perception of agents with regard to economic losses, which should vary based on the degree of conservatism. Additionally, the interference of managers—who smooth the firms' incomes to reduce the variability of earnings—can decrease the ability of stock returns to capture future economic losses included in profits or can hide the extent of the firm's risk (as measured by the variance of accounting results over time).

There are several income smoothing descriptors. The two empirical proxies of earnings smoothing more commonly used are: (1) the comparison of the variability in earnings relative to the variability of sales (or operating cash flow) and (2) the correlation between changes in accruals and changes in cash flows (Dechow, Ge, & Schrand, 2010). However, these measures do not discriminate between earnings smoothing consequence of earnings manipulation and earnings smoothing consequence of non-discretionary causes (i.e., the fundamental earnings process or the application of accounting rules). The comparison of the variability of earnings and the variability of sales has been the most widely used descriptor of smoothing behavior. Real income smoothing is reflected in sales revenue. Artificial income smoothing, on the other hand, is not reflected in sales revenue. The detection of artificial income smoothing, therefore, can be achieved by comparing the variability of earnings with the variability of sales. The variability of earnings is smaller than the variability of sales for an artificial income smoother.

3.6 Earnings Management and Accounting Conservatism

The discretionary power of managers is also reflected in the amount of conservatism. Firms can be more or less conservative in their accounting policies, and the degree of conservatism affects their accounting results. Therefore, it is important to understand how this accounting practice can affect the quality of accounting information and how it can influence EQ.

Conservatism is considered to be a major feature of financial reporting and researchers have introduced a variety of definitions of conservative accounting. Some, like Basu (1997), defined conservatism as the practice of reducing earnings (and writing down net assets) in response to "bad news" and of not increasing earnings (and writing up net assets) in response to "good news". Literature mainly refers to conservatism (biased recognition) as the understatement of assets and the overstatement of liabilities as well as the relation between the market value and the book value of the firm's (operating) assets Christensen, Feltham, & Sabac, 2005). Accounting conservatism is often expressed as "recognizing revenues and gains only when they are reasonably certain, while recognizing expenses and losses as soon as they are reasonably possible".

This principle implies that "bad news" is recognized earlier than "good news" in reported earnings, preventing managers from being overly optimistic in reporting earnings. Conservative accounting system recognizes potential decreases in income or assets' value well before they are realized and postpones the recognition of increase of income until it is realized or is sufficiently certain. Hence, conservatism is an accounting practice, consistently applied, that keeps the book values of net assets relatively low (Ruch & Taylor, 2015). For example, LIFO accounting for inventories is conservative relative to FIFO (if inventory costs are increasing); expensing research and development (R&D) expenditures rather than capitalizing and amortizing them is conservative, accelerated depreciation methods and/or using short estimated asset lives are conservative; and policies that consistently estimate high allowances for doubtful accounts, sales returns or warranty liabilities are conservative.

However, in practice, managers may take advantage of the flexibility afforded by GAAPs to subvert the conservatism intended by accounting principles. Even if a specific accounting rule is conservative, its application may not result in conservative reporting due to the subjectivity inherent in estimates (e.g., estimation of asset impairment loss). Conservative accounting raises questions about the quality of the balance sheet and the quality of earnings reported in the income statement. When the firm increases investment, conservative accounting leads to reported earnings that are lower than those that management would have done within more liberal accounting choices. These lower earnings, however, create unrecorded reserves that provide managers more flexibility to report more income in the future. Management can increase these reserves, and so reduce earnings, by increasing investment. Management can also release the reserves and create additional earnings, by subsequently reducing investment (Penman & Zhang, 2002).

The accounting for book values also affects the earnings calculation. EQ questions arise within conservative accounting because growth in investment causes earnings that are indeed lower than otherwise. But these lower earnings create "hidden reserves". Hence, hidden reserves can be increased and earnings decrease, by growing investment. Symmetrically, hidden reserves can be reduced and earnings created, by reducing investment or reducing the rate of growth in investment. If the change in investment is temporary, the induced change in earnings is also temporary, and it is not indicative of subsequent earnings.

The literature on EM is extensive, and it typically focuses on manipulation of accounting principles or accounting estimates to manage reported earnings. For example, estimates of the valuation reserve for deferred tax assets, or for doubtful accounts can be temporarily lowered to inflate earnings temporarily. Or, to reduce earnings temporarily (and to bleed them back in the future) a restructuring charge is overestimated. Accounting methods and estimates are not charges and EM is also driven by real activity. Rather, given a (conservative) accounting policy consistently applied over time, earnings are temporarily affected by (real) investment. Manipulation and EM may or may not be intended by management but, if intended, the result is achieved by the joint effect of real activity and accounting policy. The effect is perverse: The reduction of investment decreases future earnings for further investments while within conservative accounting the reduction of investment increases current earnings, making them a poor indicator of future earnings.

In research studies, conservatism has been analyzed from two perspectives so that two forms (sub-concepts) of conservatism have been conceptualized: conditional and unconditional (Ball & Shivakumar, 2005; Beaver & Ryan, 2005; Nasev, 2009).

Conditional conservatism—also labeled income statement conservatism, news-dependent conservatism, and ex-post conservatism (Ball, Kothari, & Robin, 2000; Basu, 1997; Gutiérrez & Rodríguez, 2019)—refers to the idea that earnings reflect bad news more quickly than good news (Mora & Walker, 2015); the concept of conditional conservatism can be summarized in the following phrase: “Anticipate no profit, but anticipate all losses” (Bliss, 1924). Conditional conservatism consists in the asymmetric timeliness of loss versus profit recognition, which stems from accountants’ tendency to require a higher degree of verification for recognizing good news than bad news in financial statements. Under conditional conservatism, book value is written down under sufficiently adverse circumstances, but not up under favorable ones. Hence, conditional conservatism refers to the possibility of anticipating the accounting recognition of economic losses—although not carried out—based on the negative estimates performed by management.[7] Conditional conservatism

[7] It is worth to note that this form is equivalent to recognizing economic facts in accounting with timeliness and with asymmetry, privileging evidence of negative results.

involves firms to write down the book value of net assets in a timely fashion upon receiving sufficiently bad news but not to write up net assets as quickly upon receiving correspondingly good news, with the latter being the conservative behavior.

Unconditional conservatism arises from the rule that between two alternatives of measurement and recognition of events—equally valid—you should choose the one that results in the lowest assessment of proprietors' assets.[8] Under unconditional conservatism, the book value of net assets is understated due to predetermined aspects of the accounting process.

Unconditional conservatism—also labeled balance sheet conservatism, news-independent conservatism, and ex-ante conservatism (Gutiérrez & Rodríguez, 2019)—is a pervasive bias achieved by accelerating expenses and/or delaying income recognition. In its extreme form, it causes investments to trigger expense recognition, not asset recognition (Beaver & Ryan, 2005).

Ex-ante conservatism derives from the application of GAAPs or policies that reduce earnings regardless of current economic news. As a result, these aspects of the accounting process yield expected unrecorded goodwill. Examples include the immediate expensing of advertising expenditures and R&D expenditures and other internally developed intangibles, even if they are associated with positive expected future cash flows, depreciation of property, plant and equipment that is more accelerated than economic depreciation (accelerated depreciation) and Historical Cost Accounting (HCA) for positive net present value projects.

Unconditional conservatism occurs ex-ante, i.e., assets are valued below their current value on an ongoing basis, which will not affect the market value of the shares. One can then infer that unconditional conservatism interferes with the ability of economic agents in the capital market to distinguish an economic loss during a given period from the occurrence of continuous losses or from the undervaluation of assets. This condition is directly related to the anticipation or deferral of revenues and expenditures.

Accounting information is continually influenced by risks, uncertainties and, above all, economic factors. Conservatism can impair the measurement of economic reality by imposing the smallest value between two

[8] Prudence is the purpose of unconditional conservatism, and it is related to the degree of uncertainty about the derivative effects of transactions initiated.

available alternatives. Financial adjustments that depreciate asset are most often reflected in firms' accounting results, for example, via provisions for loan losses, adjustments to asset depreciation rates, or losses raised by impairment tests. These accounting choices are subjective and are directly related to the degree of discretion of those who draft the financial statements.

In general, both conditional conservatism and income smoothing are properties of accounting information that are directly related to and influence the quality of the accounting information that is disclosed to the market. The reduction of optimism in the results disclosed is theoretically a feature of accounting conservatism; however, in this case, reduced optimism can also be a consequence of income smoothing practices that are intended to prevent profits from appearing to be too far above or below market expectations. Therefore, both of these practices, conservatism and smoothing, can result in a reduction of optimism.

3.7 Earnings Management and Earnings Informativeness

The earnings informativeness has received considerable attention in recent times and continues to be a challenging issue for investors, financial analysts, management, regulators, and academic researchers. Earnings informativeness can be defined as the amount of information about future earnings or future cash flows stored in the current-period stock return (Zarowin, 2002). The need to ascertain how and why accounting numbers—especially earnings—express a firm's market or economic value drives the investigation of earnings informativeness. Investment decisions in financial markets are influenced by information resources and especially financial statements are one useful source of data from the viewpoint of stock exchange theorists. One of the most important factors in financial reporting is the announcement of information related to earnings, which has probably attracted the highest rate of attention from investors in order to facilitate their decision-making. The verification and measurement rules underlying financial reporting, along with the scrutiny by fiduciary agents such as auditors and board of directors, are generally thought to make earnings informative (Ball & Shivakumar, 2005, 2008). In this regard, earnings informativeness refers to the extent of reaction of economic or market value to accounting disclosures.[9]

It is important to realize that EM plays an essential beneficial role as a means for managers to reveal their private information (Jiraporn & Miller, 2008). When EM is used as a vehicle for the communication of management's inside information to investors, the somewhat surprising conclusion is that a little bit of EM can be "good". Managers can use accounting judgment to make financial reports more informative for users. This can arise if certain accounting choices or estimates are perceived to be credible signals of a firm's financial performance. In this case, management communicates its private information about the firm's performance through financial reporting (Arya, Glover, & Sunder, 2003; Beaver & Ryan, 2005; Fields, Lys, & Vincent, 2001). In seeking of the wholly fairness, accounting information's users tend to rely on income statement primarily as an extremely important tool for assessing the quality of earnings. The income statement can be the perfect tool for generating information about companies and disclosing the success of their operations, if it is not affected by accrual-based EM (i.e., EM through a change in the accrual process or a deviation from normal business activity within GAAPs accounting choices that try to obscure or to mask true economic performance) (Boghdady, 2019; Enomoto, Kimura, & Yamaguchi, 2015).

Sometimes managers choose carefully the methods helping them to disclose desired information regarding their companies' performance. The result could be an increase or a decrease in the income figures that provides a smooth trend of the income in the long run, offering a strong and stable image for the company, especially in times of financial crisis.

EM is closely associated with the information transparency and the information asymmetry that comprise EQ. Thus, EM represents a crucial factor affecting EQ. EM may lead stakeholders to make decisions based on unreliable information, eventually leading to inefficiency of investment (Cormier, Houle, & Ledoux, 2013) and, therefore, it is expected to be inversely related to EQ. This is the case of pervasive use of financial information revealing less reliable information to influence decision-making of stakeholders and achieving benefits for managers of the firm (Cheng &

[9] The first strong evidence on the reaction of stock markets to the declaration and publication of earnings' information was provided by Ball and Brown (1968). This research indicated that reactions of investors to firms with bad news resulted in negative unexpected abnormal returns.

Warfield, 2005; Dechow & Skinner, 2000; Healy & Wahlen, 1999). Managers can also use their judgment in financial reporting and in structuring transactions to alter financial reports to either mislead some stakeholders about the underlying economic performance of the company or to influence contractual outcomes that depend on reported accounting numbers. In this case, management uses its private information to distort signals about firm performance through financial reporting, undermining annual report readability (Lo, Ramos, & Rogo, 2017).

There are many ways that managers can follow to exercise judgment in financial reporting. For example, judgment is required to estimate numerous future economic events, such as expected lives and salvage values of long-term assets, obligations for pension benefits and other post-employment benefits, deferred taxes, and losses from bad debts and assets impairments. Managers must also choose among acceptable accounting methods for reporting the same economic transactions, e.g., the straight-line or accelerated depreciation methods or the LIFO, FIFO, or weighted-average inventory valuation methods. In addition, managers must exercise judgment in working capital management (e.g., inventory levels, the timing of inventory shipments or purchases, and receivable policies), which affects cost allocations and net revenues. Managers must also choose to make or defer expenditures, such as R&D, advertising or maintenance. Finally, they must decide how to structure corporate transactions.

EM is primarily realized by managers to achieve desired earnings' amounts through accounting choices among GAAPs by discretionary accruals manipulations or/and the manipulation of the operating activities of a company. Reliability of earnings becomes questionable when managers have an incentive to manipulate reported earnings opportunistically. Such manipulations alter shareholders' perception of the reliability of reported earnings due to the increase in the level of non-permanent components included in total earnings.

However, key questions are how far management should go in helping investors to form rational expectations about firm's performance through their accruals choices and when does this activity become EM? Because accounting is inherently subjective, application of judgment in a benign way without the aim of personal gain is not considered to be EM. Accruals allow earnings to provide better information about economic performance to investors than cash flows do.

There are remaining questions about the role of accruals in improving EQ to assist the users of financial reports in predicting future performance. Regarding the role of accruals in financial accounting, the existing accounting literature investigated whether earnings smoothing through discretionary accruals improves or deteriorates the informativeness of earnings. Although the effect of income smoothing on earnings informativeness is not thoroughly investigated, the accounting literature so far theorizes two opposite effects of income smoothing on earnings informativeness (Bertomeu et al., 2016; Beyer et al., 2019; Tucker & Zarowin, 2006; Zarowin, 2002). Managers can make discretionary accounting choices that are considered either a practice of efficient communication of private information or distorting disclosure. It is a question of assessing whether EM is opportunistic or informative since managerial discretion is used either to distort earnings' informativeness or to convey useful information to investors.

One viewpoint is that managers use income smoothing to make public their private information about the firm's future earnings. When income smoothing is used to communicate private information about future performance expectations, it could provide more information about future earnings and cash flows, which in turn is reflected in the stock prices. Here, both discretionary and non-discretionary accrual accounting practices increase the informativeness of earnings. If discretionary accruals predict future cash flows, managers can use them to signal their private information rather than to manipulate them opportunistically. About the role of discretionary accruals for the usefulness of earnings, there are two hypotheses in positive accounting theory: signaling and opportunism. According to the signaling perspective, discretionary accruals can improve the information content of earnings by allowing managers to signal their private information about future cash flows. Reporting earnings that correspond more closely to economic performance is one of the numerous possible benefits of intentional smoothing, if it does not reflect opportunistic behavior (Demerjian, Lewis-Western, & McVay, 2017). In this regard, high ability of managers in incorporating more forward-looking information about cash flows into current earnings through smoothing, can enhance the informativeness of earnings and stock prices about future performance. Accounting Standard Setters, in fact, argue that forecasting future cash flows is one of the key objectives of financial reporting, as well it is fundamental to a firm's financial valuation. The alternative perspective instead suggests that income smoothing alters information and makes stock prices less informative. According to the opportunism hypothesis, discretionary accruals can be used opportunistically, and thus they can distort the information of earnings. If income smoothing is distorting, then the resulting earnings are less informative about future ones. Less information about the future earnings and cash flows will be reflected in the stock prices, making smoothing damaging. These conceptualizations of EM describes reasonable and proper practices that are part of a managed business that delivers value of stakeholders or protects management interest.

3.8 Earnings Quality and Earnings Management

EM and EQ can be regarded as two of the most attractive and challenging issues in accounting. In prior literature, numerous definitions have been developed for EQ and in many studies it has been closely related to EM (Teets, 2002). Sometimes EM is almost used as a synonym for EQ; for example, Abdelghany (2005) discussed EQ and its measures as aspects of EM. However, it is important to note that EQ is definitely another concept than EM—as further explained below—but it can be seen as an aspect influencing EQ. EM affects EQ as highly managed earnings have low quality. However, the lack of EM is not sufficient to guarantee high-quality earnings (or high-quality accounting numbers more generally), because other factors contribute to the quality of earnings (Lo, 2008).

Put another way, financial statements' users may also define EQ in terms of the "absence of earnings management". This is because the intentional manipulation of earnings ended by managers, within the limits allowed by the Accounting Standards, may distort the usefulness of earnings to users. Persistent and predictable earnings may not be of high quality if they result from EM. Managers may tend to manage earnings for a number of reasons—including those related to capital market motivations, compensation, and bonus as well as debt or lending contracts—which will result in low quality of earnings. Debt agreements based on low and defective earnings could induce unintended wealth transfers, overstated earnings as an indicator of managers' performance could result in overcompensation to managers in compensation contracts and low quality of earnings may provide faulty resource allocation signals to investors.

There are three different types of decisions that can affect the quality of earnings: decisions made by Standard Setters, management's choices of accounting methods and management's judgments and estimates in applying the Accounting Standards. The role of management's decisions is important for the quality of earnings as well as the application of Accounting Standards have an impact on the quality of earnings. Our precision-based perspective on EQ is related to EM because management's financial reporting decisions are one of several determinants of EQ. It is important to note that certain decisions, e.g., opportunistic discretion of managers in determining accounting amounts, have an impact on the quality of earnings. For example, earnings smoothing, by others, is related to EM. In particular, income smoothing can improve or impair the quality of earnings since it is a form of EM. Theoretically, if quality of earnings is improved, then the association between firm value and reported earnings should also be improved.

Prior literature documented that EM erodes EQ (Arthur, Tang, & Lin, 2015; Healy & Wahlen, 1999) as it implies earnings opacity and information risk. If we define EM as the intentional intervention in the financial reporting process in an attempt to obtain some advantage from them (Schipper, 1989), we can suppose that the decrease of EQ is a consequence of EM. Given the information asymmetry and the conflict of interests between insiders (e.g., managers and controlling owners) and stakeholders, managers have the opportunity to disclose financial information in the most favorable way for them to the detriment of the external users' interests (Beyer et al., 2019; Ghazali, Shafie, & Sanusi, 2015). For example, managers can use their discretion in preparing financial reports to maximize earnings and cover losses or to understate earnings in years of good performance, creating reserves in order to mask the variability of earnings. Managers have a lot of incentives to manipulate earnings but the effect of these different incentives on earnings hasn't a specific pattern (Iatridis & Dimitras, 2013). In addition, the earnings-based compensation of managers is also pointed out as one of the reasons for them to engage in EM. Furthermore, firms may manipulate earnings to meet (or to beat) analysts' expectations (Khaled, 2005; Persakis & Iatridis, 2015) and hence to influence the stock price. EM has a negative effect on the quality of earnings if it distorts the information in a way that it becomes less useful for predicting future cash flows. As the term "quality of earnings" refers to the credibility of the earnings number reported, EM reduces the reliability of income in this circumstance. Moreover, the practice of EM damages the perceived quality of reported earnings over the entire market in this case, resulting in the belief that reported earnings do not reflect economic reality. This will eventually lead to unnecessary stock price fluctuation and ultimately this uncertainty may have the potential to undermine the efficient flow of capital, thereby damaging the markets as a whole.

From a different point of view, there is evidence in the literature (Bertomeu et al., 2016; Demerjian, Lev, Lewis, & McVay, 2013) that financial analysts associate high EQ with the ability of a company's managers to manage earnings in order to avoid negative earnings surprises. So, they consider that a company has high quality of earnings when it has discretionary reserves, allowances, or off-balance-sheet assets, which can be modified if actual results are below predictions. In this regard, managers can use their managerial ability to improve the quality of estimates and judgments to form earnings (EQ) by fewer subsequent restatements, lower errors in the bad debt provisions, higher accruals persistence and higher quality accrual estimations (Huang & Sun, 2017).

There is also another characteristic of using EM as a measure of EQ. As indicated in prior literature on EQ (Teets, 2002), EM is often linked to EQ and although they are different concepts, there is a reason for this coupling between EQ and EM. Regarding this relation and how management decision can affect EQ, we argue that EM would indicate less bias in the earnings and therefore higher quality of earnings. In this respect, we note that the effect of EM on the precision of earnings as a descriptor of an underlying construct is likely to be highly context-specific. Investors are more interested in buying the shares of companies whose incomes are more stable. Moreover, investors believe that companies reporting high levels of fluctuation take more risks in comparison with those reporting smooth earnings. Considering this issue, managers are inclined to level the earnings of their companies in order to visualize them with high levels of stability in earnings.

Bibliography

Abdelghany, K. E. (2005). Measuring the quality of earnings. *Managerial Auditing Journal, 20*(9), 1001–1015.

Alhadab, M., Clacher, I., & Keasey, K. (2015). Real and accrual earnings management and IPO failure risk. *Accounting and Business Research, 45*(1), 55–92.

Ali, A., & Zhang, W. (2015). CEO tenure and earnings management. *Journal of Accounting and Economics, 59*(1), 60–79.

Arthur, N., Tang, Q., & Lin, Z. (2015). Corporate accruals quality during the 2008–2010 global financial crisis. *Journal of International Accounting, Auditing and Taxation, 25*(C), 1–15.

Arya, A., Glover, J. C., & Sunder, S. (2003). Are unmanaged earnings always better for shareholders? *Accounting Horizons, 17*(s–1), 111–116.

Baik, B., Choi, S., Farber, D. B. (2019, October 11). Managerial ability and income smoothing. *The Accounting Review*. Available at: https://doi.org/10.2308/accr-52600.

Ball, R., & Brown, P. (1968). An empirical evaluation of accounting income numbers. *Journal of Accounting Research, 6*(2), 159–178.

Ball, R., Kothari, S. P., & Robin, A. (2000). The effect of international institutional factors on properties of accounting earnings. *Journal of Accounting and Economics, 29*(1), 1–51.

Ball, R., & Shivakumar, L. (2005). Earnings quality in UK private firms: Comparative loss recognition timeliness. *Journal of Accounting and Economics, 39*(1), 83–128.

Ball, R., & Shivakumar, L. (2008). Earnings quality at initial public offerings. *Journal of Accounting and Economics, 45*(2–3), 324–349.

Barth, M. E., Landsman, W. R., & Lang, M. H. (2008). International accounting standards and accounting quality. *Journal of Accounting Research, 46*(3), 467–498.

Basu, S. (1997). The conservatism principle and the asymmetric timeliness of earnings. *Journal of Accounting and Economics, 24*(1), 3–37.

Beaver, W. H., & Ryan, S. G. (2005). Conditional and unconditional conservatism: Concepts and modeling. *Review of Accounting Studies, 10*(2–3), 269–309.

Beidleman, C. R. (1973). Income smoothing: The role of management. *The Accounting Review, 48*(4), 653–667.

Bertomeu, J., Ma, P., & Marinovic, I. (2016). How often do managers withhold information? *SSRN Electronic Journal*, online publication date: 1 January 2016.

Beyer, A., Guttman, I., & Marinovic, I. (2019). Earnings management and earnings quality: Theory and evidence. *The Accounting Review, 94*(4), 77–101.

Biddle, G. C., & Hilary, G. (2006). Accounting quality and firm-level capital investment. *The Accounting Review, 81*(5), 963–982.

Bliss, J. H. (1924). *Management through accounts.* New York: The Ronald Press Co.

Boghdady, A. B. A. (2019). Accrual and real earnings management in both state-owned and privately-owned Egyptian companies. *Corporate Ownership & Control, 17*(1), 8–13.

Capkun, V., Collins, D., & Jeanjean, T. (2016). The effect of IAS/IFRS adoption on earnings management (smoothing): A closer look at competing explanations. *Journal of Accounting and Public Policy, 35*(4), 352–394.

Carmo, C., Moreira, J., & Miranda, M. (2016). Earnings quality and cost of debt: Evidence from Portuguese private companies. *Journal of Financial Reporting and Accounting, 14*(2), 178–197.

Cheng, Q., & Warfield, T. D. (2005). Equity incentives and earnings management. *The Accounting Review, 80*(2), 441–476.

Cheng, Q., Warfield, T. D., & Ye, M. (2011). Equity incentives and earnings management: Evidence from the banking industry. *Journal of Accounting, Auditing and Finance, 26*(2), 317–349.

Chiraz, D., & Anis, J. (2013). Earnings management and performance of French IPO companies. *Journal of Accounting and Taxation, 5*(1), 1–14.

Christensen, P. O., Feltham, G. A., & Sabac, F. (2005). A contracting perspective on earnings quality. *Journal of Accounting and Economics, 39*(2), 265–294.

Cormier, D., Houle, S., & Ledoux, M. J. (2013). The incidence of earnings management on information asymmetry in an uncertain environment: Some Canadian evidence. *Journal of International Accounting, Auditing and Taxation, 22*(1), 26–38.

Dechow, P. M. (1994). Accounting earnings and cash flows as measures of firm performance: The role of accounting accruals. *Journal of Accounting and Economics, 18*(1), 3–42.

Dechow, P. M., Ge, W., & Schrand, C. (2010). Understanding earnings quality: A review of the proxies, their determinants and their consequences. *Journal of Accounting and Economics, 50*(2–3), 344–401.

Dechow, P. M., Kothari, S. P., & Watts, R. L. (1998). The relation between earnings and cash flows. *Journal of Accounting and Economics, 25*(2), 133–168.

Dechow, P. M., & Skinner, D. J. (2000). Earnings management: Reconciling the views of accounting academics. *Practitioners, and Regulators, Accounting Horizons, 14*(2), 235–250.

Dechow, P. M., Sloan, R. G., & Sweeney, A. P. (1995). Detecting earnings management. *The Accounting Review, 70*(2), 193–225.

Demerjian, P. R., Lev, B., Lewis, M. F., & McVay, S. E. (2013). Managerial ability and earnings quality. *The Accounting Review, 88*(2), 463–498.

Demerjian, P. R., Lewis-Western, M., & McVay, S. (2017). How does intentional earnings smoothing vary with managerial ability. Conference Submission, *Journal of Accounting, Auditing & Finance*, 1–32.

Dutta, S., & Gigler, F. (2002). The effect of earnings forecasts on earnings management. *Journal of Accounting Research, 40*(3), 631–655.

Enomoto, M., Kimura, F., & Yamaguchi, T. (2015, May). *Accrual-based and real earnings management: An international comparison for investor protection* (Discussion Paper Series). RIEB, Kobe University, 1–38.

Fields, T. D., Lys, T. Z., & Vincent, L. (2001). Empirical research on accounting choice. *Journal of Accounting and Economics, 31*(1–3), 255–307.

Francis, J., LaFond, R., Olsson, P. M., & Schipper, K. (2004). Costs of equity and earnings attributes. *The Accounting Review, 79*(4), 967–1010.

Francis, J., Olsson, P., & Schipper, K. (2008). Earnings quality. *Foundations and Trends in Accounting, 1*(4), 259–340.

Gao, J., Cong, L. M., & Evans, J. (2015). Earnings management, IPO underpricing, and post-issue stock performance of Chinese SMEs. *The Chinese Economy, 48*(5), 351–371.

Gassen, J., Fülbier, R. U., & Sellhorn, T. (2006). International differences in conditional conservatism—The role of unconditional conservatism and income smoothing. *European Accounting Review, 15*(4), 527–564.

Ge, W., & Kim, J. B. (2014). Real earnings management and the cost of new corporate bonds. *Journal of Business Research, 67*(4), 641–647.

Ghazali, A. W., Shafie, N. A., & Sanusi, Z. M. (2015). Earnings management: An analysis of opportunistic behaviour, monitoring mechanism and financial distress. *Procedia Economics and Finance, 28*, 190–201.

Giroux, G. (2003). *Detecting earnings management*. New York: Wiley.

Goel, A., & Thakor, A. V. (2003). Why do firms smooth earnings? *The Journal of Business, 76*(1), 151–192.

Graham, J. R., Harvey, C., & Rajgopal, S. (2005). The economic implications of corporate financial reporting. *Journal of Accounting and Economics, 40*(1–3), 3–73.

Gutiérrez, A. L., & Rodríguez, M. C. (2019). A review on the multidimensional analysis of earnings quality. *Spanish Accounting Review, 22*(1), 41–60.

Healy, P. M., & Wahlen, J. M. (1999). A review of the earnings management literature and its implications for standard setting. *Accounting Horizons, 13*(4), 365–383.

Huang, X. S., & Sun, L. (2017). Managerial ability and real earnings management. *Advances in Accounting, 39*, 91–104.

Iatridis, G., & Dimitras, A. I. (2013). Financial crisis and accounting quality: Evidence from five European countries. *Advances in Accounting, 29*(1), 154–160.

Imhoff, E. A. (1981). Income smoothing: An analysis of critical issues. *Quarterly Review of Economics and Business, 21*(Autumn), 23–42.

Indjejikian, R. J. (2014). Earnings targets and annual bonus incentives. *The Accounting Review, 89*(4), 1227–1258.

Jaggi, B., & Lee, P. (2002). Earnings management response to debt covenant violations and debt restructuring. *Journal of Accounting, Auditing & Finance, 17*(4), 295–324.

Jiraporn, P., & Miller, G. A. (2008). Is earnings management opportunistic or beneficial? An agency theory perspective. *International Review of Financial Analysis, 17*(3), 622–634.

Jones, C. E., Clark, S. J., & Vann, C. E. (2007). Using goodwill impairment to effect earnings management during SFAS No. 142's year of adoption and later. *Journal of Business and Economic Research, 5*(1), 23–30.

Kanagaretnam, K., Lim, C., & Lobo, G. (2014). Influence of national culture on accounting conservatism and risk-taking in the banking industry. *The Accounting Review, 89*(3), 1115–1149.

Khaled, E. A. (2005). Measuring the quality of earnings. *Managerial Auditing Journal, 20*(9), 1001–1015.

Leuz, C., Nanda, D., & Wyscocki, P. D. (2003). Earnings management and investor protection: An international comparison. *Journal of Financial Economics, 69*(3), 505–527.

Lo, K. (2008). Earnings management and earnings quality. *Journal of Accounting and Economics, 45*(2–3), 350–357.

Lo, K., Ramos, F., & Rogo, R. (2017). Earnings management and annual report readability. *Journal of Accounting and Economics, 63*(1), 1–25.

Matsumoto, D. A. (2002). Management's incentives to avoid negative earnings surprises. *The Accounting Review, 77*(3), 483–514.

Mora, A., & Walker, M. (2015). The implications of research on accounting conservatism for accounting standard setting. *Accounting and Business Research, 45*(5), 620–650.

Nagata, K. (2013). Does earnings management lead to favorable IPO price formation or further underpricing? Evidence from Japan. *Journal of Multinational Financial Management, 23*(4), 301–313.

Nasev, J. (2009). *Conditional and unconditional conservatism: Implications for accounting based valuation and risky projects.* Wiesbaden: Gabler, GWV Fachverlage GmbH.

Penman, S. H., & Zhang, X.-J. (2002). Accounting conservatism, the quality of earnings, and stock returns. *The Accounting Review, 77*(2), 237–264.

Persakis, A., & Iatridis, G. E. (2015). Earnings quality under financial crisis: A global empirical investigation. *Journal of Multinational Financial Management, 30*(C), 1–35.

Ronen, J., & Yaari, V. (2008). *Earnings management: Emerging insights in theory, practice and research.* New York: Springer.

Ruch, G. W., & Taylor, G. (2015). Accounting conservatism: A review of the literature. *Journal of Accounting Literature, 34*(1), 17–38.

Schipper, K. (1989). Commentary on earnings management. *Accounting Horizons, 3*(4), 91–102.
Shaw, K. W. (2003). Corporate disclosure quality, earnings smoothing, and earnings' timeliness. *Journal of Business Research, 56*(12), 1043–1050.
Shen, C. H., & Huang, Y. L. (2013). Effects of earnings management on bank cost of debt. *Accounting & Finance, 53*(1), 265–300.
Shuto, A. (2007). Executive compensation and earnings management: Empirical evidence from Japan. *Journal of International Accounting, Auditing and Taxation, 16*, 1–26.
Siegel, J. G. (1982). The "quality of earnings" concept: A survey. *Financial Analysts Journal, 38*(2), 60–68.
Stanga, K., & Kelton, A. (2007). Managerial intent and the ethics of earnings management. In C. Jeffrey (Ed.), *Research on professional responsibility and ethics in accounting* (Vol. 12, pp. 149–172). Bingley: Emerald Group Publishing Limited.
Teets, R. W. (2002). Quality of earnings: An introduction to the issues in accounting education [Special issue]. *Issues in Accounting Education, 17*(4), 335–360.
Teshima, N., & Shuto, A. (2008). Managerial ownership and earnings management: Theory and empirical evidence from Japan. *Journal of International Financial Management and Accounting, 19*(2), 139–160.
Tucker, J., & Zarowin, P. (2006). Does income smoothing improve earnings informativeness? *The Accounting Review, 81*(1), 251–270.
Van Tendeloo, B. V., & Vanstraelen, A. (2005). Earnings management under German Gaap versus IFRS. *European Accounting Review, 14*(1), 155–180.
Zarowin, P. (2002). *Does income smoothing make stock prices more informative?* (NYU Working Paper No. 2451/27592). New York University.

CHAPTER 4

IAS/IFRSs, Accounting Quality and Earnings Quality

Abstract The effect of IAS/IFRSs on accounting quality has been a subject of the international research agenda for many years. Some researchers argued that IAS/IFRSs improves the reliability of financial reporting by limiting opportunistic managerial discretion while others claimed that the accounting flexibility of IAS/IFRSs might provide greater opportunities for earnings manipulation. The question focused on both the degree of EM and the value relevance of reported earnings in the context of IAS/IFRSs. An increase in EM could have a positive effect on EQ when managers engage in EM in order to communicate private information. However, the use of IAS/IFRSs may increase managerial discretionary behaviors and opportunistic EM making the economic consequence of IAS/IFRSs adoption complicated.

Keywords IAS/IFRSs · Accounting quality · Earnings quality (EQ) · Accounting Standards · Financial reporting

4.1 Introduction

Financial reporting is the main source of information used by investors, creditors, lenders, and other stakeholders in making economic decisions.

E. Menicucci, *Earnings Quality*,
https://doi.org/10.1007/978-3-030-36798-5_4

According to the communication theory,[1] Financial statements are one of the main managers' means to communicate information about a firm's financial conditions and economic results to the market. High quality of financial reporting information is important because it positively influences capital providers and other stakeholders in making investments and resource allocation decisions enhancing overall market efficiency.

In fact, according to the Conceptual Framework for Financial Reporting amended by the IASB (2010, 2018),[2] the primary objective of financial reporting is to provide high-quality useful information to present and potential capital providers (equity investors, lenders, and other creditors) in making decisions in their capacity as capital providers. The goal of this International Standards Setter has been to define a set of high-quality standards that can provide comparable and transparent information to the users of financial reporting. In line with this Conceptual Framework, we similarly define financial reporting quality in terms of decision usefulness.

Although both the FASB and the IASB stress the importance of high-quality financial reports, one of the key problems is how to operationalize and measure this quality. Because of its context-specificity, an empirical assessment of financial reporting quality inevitably includes preferences among a myriad of constituents (Botosan, 2004; Daske & Gebhardt, 2006; Dechow & Dichev, 2002; Schipper & Vincent, 2003). Since different users have dissimilar preferences, the same quality could diverge among constituents. In addition, the users may also perceive differently the usefulness of similar information due to their particular context. As a result of these user-specific settings, the valuation of quality directly seems problematic (Botosan, 2004). Consequently, many researchers measure the quality of financial reporting indirectly by focusing on attributes that

[1] According to communication theory, analysis of corporate financial disclosures can provide useful information to stakeholders. Communication is a goal-directed activity that involves a purpose. One of the central goals of communication for a company is to maintain a positive image.

[2] The revised Conceptual Framework for Financial Reporting (Conceptual Framework) issued in March 2018 is effective immediately for the International Accounting Standards Board (Board) and the IFRS Interpretations Committee. The Conceptual Framework sets out the fundamental concepts for financial reporting that guide the Board in developing IFRS Standards. It helps to ensure that the Standards are conceptually consistent and that similar transactions are treated the same way, so as to provide useful information for investors, lenders, and other creditors. The Conceptual Framework also assists companies in developing accounting policies when no IFRS Standard applies to a particular transaction, and more broadly, helps stakeholders to understand and interpret the Standards.

are believed to influence quality of financial reports, such as EM and timeliness (Barth, Landsman, & Lang, 2008; Cohen, Krishnamoorthy, & Wright, 2004; Nichols & Wahlen, 2004; Schipper & Vincent, 2003).

Despite a considerable interest on the effectiveness of Accounting Standards in improving the quality of financial reporting, empirical literature offered contradictory findings about the question to what extent Accounting Standards contribute to the decision usefulness of financial reporting information. Increased level of disclosure in corporate financial reports could affect the quality of reported earnings. As more disclosure is required, any attempts to manage earnings can easily be detected and reduced by internal monitoring bodies (board of directors and auditors) in a company. Moreover, a disclosure system that is founded on high-quality Standards develops the investors' confidence in the credibility of financial reporting (Levitt, 1998).

The application of IAS/IFRSs and its impact on accounting quality have been a topic of the international research agenda for a number of years. Many studies documented that the adoption of high-quality Accounting Standards results in an increasing quality of accounting information. For example, some researchers claimed that IAS/IFRSs improves the reliability of financial reporting by limiting opportunistic managerial discretion (Barth et al., 2008; Ewert & Wagenhofer, 2010). On the contrary, other researchers argued that the flexibility inherent in IAS/IFRSs might provide greater opportunities for managers to manipulate earnings (Burgstahler, Hail, & Leuz, 2006; Street & Gray, 2002).

To examine the effect of IAS/IFRSs' adoption on EQ, we investigate whether both the level of EM is significantly lower and the reported earnings are more value relevant due to the use of these Accounting Standards. In short, we study whether the application of IAS/IFRSs is associated with high accounting quality, less EM, more timely loss recognition and high value relevance of accounting figures.

4.2 Accounting Standards and Accounting Quality

There is no single, widely accepted, specific definition of the term "accounting quality" and despite the increased attention on it, this term is vague and difficult to define. In literature, the concept is presented somewhat different in many papers and it is personalized to the aim of research. Accounting quality is challenging to detect and there is no consensus also on the best way to measure it. In practice, definitions of accounting quality vary significantly across individuals, projects, researchers, and organizations.

Many different definitions of accounting quality can be found in literature. In most of the papers (Barth et al., 2008; Soderstrom & Sun, 2007), accounting quality is defined either as quality of financial statements (financial reporting) or by qualitative characteristics of financial information (according to IAS/IFRSs or US GAAPs). Particularly, we can define it as either the precision with which financial reporting is useful in predicting future performance or the extent to which accounting information accurately reflects the company's current operating performance. Although there are many definitions of accounting quality, they all ultimately serve the same purpose: to enable stakeholders in making value judgments about accounting information.

Anyway, we agree with Hribar, Kravet, and Wilson (2014) that it is difficult to define and measure accounting quality due to its complexity and its various connotations. In general, users perceive a product (i.e., financial information presented in the financial statements of an entity) having a high degree of quality if it meets their expectations and it satisfies their information needs. In this regard, financial reports are one of the major mediums by which information is disseminated to the external users. Since information is crucial in this process, it is important to ensure that the financial reports, and the numbers therein, convey high-quality financial information to the users. High-quality information reduces agency problems by closing the information asymmetry[3] gap that exists between management and shareholders and in doing so, it is critical to the proper functioning of capital markets (Shaw, 2003). Penman's notion of accounting quality is based on the usefulness of information for the shareholders (Penman, 2003) as he considers that accounting quality should be discussed in terms of shareholders' interests and fair valuation of those interests. Under this perspective, accounting should promote shareholders' interest but it should also consider the public interest.

High-quality accounting information plays an important disclosure role within the financial market in this regard, as it gives an appropriate and

[3] Information asymmetry refers to the fact that management has inside information about the true economic status of the firm that they may or may not share with stakeholders.

transparent disclosure about firms' conditions and results of their operations. The transparency that it can be achieved with high-quality information leads to a reduction of information asymmetry as it is able to grant a faithful and truthful representation of firms' accounting results (Brown & Hillegeist, 2007). Namely, earnings can be considered as a performance measure for shareholders to monitor management, given the interests' conflict between management and shareholders. Moreover, financial reporting is typically contended as having an important stewardship role that is focused on assessing managerial performance (Ribeiro, Shan, & Taylor, 2019; Ronen & Yaari, 2008).[4] A company's commitment to disclose private information results in significant benefits in terms of capital cost and major market efficiency (Armstrong, Core, Taylore, & Verrecchia, 2011; Lambert, Leuz, & Verrecchia, 2007, 2012; Leuz & Verrecchia, 2000). For that reason, accounting quality is of great interest to participants in the financial reporting supply chain. For example, better accounting quality can translate into a lower cost of capital to a reporting entity while better accounting quality can translate into a more profitable allocation of capital to an investor.

As capital markets rely on financial accounting information, it must be relevant and credible. Summarizing various comments on the concept, we define accounting quality—similar to Hribar et al. (2014)—as the degree of usefulness of accounting information to represent a true and fair view of entity's financial results and position, to predict its future performance and to enhance assessment of entity's value.

The central concept of accounting quality is that some accounting information is better than other in disclosing what it purports to communicate. Credible information means that it is—as much as possible—a true representation of a firm's financial situation, as well as complete, neutral and free from errors. Basic factors that determine high-quality financial reporting numbers include each country's legal and political environment, financial reporting incentives, and applied Accounting Standards. Further, the quality of accounting information is strongly linked to how firm performance is measured. Therefore, any improvement of the quality of accounting information should provide better tools for the valuation of the firm, and consequently it increases the efficiency and the

[4]The IASB removed the stewardship term from the 2010 Conceptual Framework, but it is now explicitly recognized in the 2018 version.

reliability of capital markets. To sum up, quality of accounting information can be useful for valuation purposes as well as for performance evaluation, contracting, or stewardship purposes (Kothari, Leone, & Charles, 2005).

The majority of literature reveals that accounting quality is analyzed along with the transition from one set of Accounting Standards to another or specifically with the use of IAS/IFRSs (Armstrong, Barth, Jagolinzer, & Riedl, 2010; Barth et al., 2008; Soderstrom & Sun, 2007). However, little research has directly addressed the impact of IAS/IFRSs' adoption on the financial reporting quality and assessment of changes in quality moving from national to international Accounting Standards (i.e., IAS/IFRSs) is mixed. The improvement of the information environment following the implementation of IAS/IFRSs is based upon the premise that these Accounting Standards induce higher quality of financial reporting. The adoption of IAS/IFRSs implies less EM, more timely loss recognition, and more value relevance of earnings, all of which are an evidence of high accounting quality (Cormier & Magnan, 2016). We share the idea that IAS/IFRSs assure more accurate, comprehensive and prosperous financial statement information, relative to the national Standards. Consistent with these characteristics of high-quality accounting, prior research suggested that high-quality earnings are more value relevant (Lang, Ready, & Wilson, 2006; Lang, Ready, & Yetman, 2003; Leuz, Nanda, & Wyscocki, 2003).

Concerning the value relevance, it is assumed that high accounting quality determined a close association between stock prices and equity book value because earnings of higher quality better reflect a firm's underlying economics (Okafor & Warsame, 2016). In this regard, high-quality accounting results from applying Accounting Standards that faithfully represent a firm's underlying economics. Additionally, high-quality accounting is less affected by opportunistic managerial discretion and has less non-opportunistic error in estimating accruals (Iatridis, 2011).

As defined in the IASB Conceptual Framework for Financial Reporting (2010, 2018), a financial information is useful if it is relevant (have a predictive value and/or a confirmatory value) and it is faithfully represented (be completed, neutral, and free from error). The information presented in financial statements must have the characteristics of relevance and representational faithfulness in order to meet the objectives of financial reporting. These fundamental qualitative characteristics (i.e., relevance and faithful representation) are the most important dimensions of information and they determine the content and the quality of financial reporting.

4.2.1 *Qualitative Characteristics and the Quality of Financial Reporting*

To determine the quality and the decision usefulness of financial reporting information, we refer to prior literature which describes financial reporting quality in terms of the fundamental and enhancing qualitative characteristics as proposed in the IASB Conceptual Framework for Financial Reporting (IASB, 2010, 2018). Instead of defining quality, the IASB Framework lists a number of qualitative characteristics that should allow to achieve a high-quality information, i.e., relevance, faithful representation, comparability, verifiability, timeliness, and understandability.[5] The FASB Conceptual Framework instead refers to the reliability (or truthfulness) of financial statements and to the relevance and predictive ability of information presented in financial statements.

According to the IASB, high-quality accounting information comprises several qualities but it implies two primary qualities of information: relevance and reliability. Both the Conceptual Frameworks place emphasis on similar characteristics in determining the quality of information but it can be drawn that relevance and reliability are the key characteristics of information quality. Looking at the different aspects of both reliability and relevance, these two qualitative characteristics result in multiple items that refer to the sub notions of them.

The relevance characteristic means that the information is capable of making a difference when it is used by various users and in different users' decisions-making process (Soderstrom & Sun, 2007). Relevant information influences the economic decisions of users by helping them to evaluate past, present, and future events or by confirming or correcting their past evaluations. Hence, the common aspect of the relevance dimension is the ability of information to help users in predicting or in confirming expectations. Two elements of relevance are materiality and timeliness. The information is material if the decision of the user is affected by the omission or misstatement of that information. The information is timely if it is provided to users within a time period in which the decision of the

[5] While avoiding a formal definition of EQ, the initial Conceptual Framework joint project undertaken by the Financial Accounting Standards Board (FASB) and the International Accounting Standards Board (IASB) lists qualitative characteristics that should achieve high quality, including relevance, faithful representation, comparability, verifiability, timeliness, and understandability.

user will be affected. In other words, timeliness means that the information is available when it is needed, i.e., it means having information available to decision-makers before it loses its capacity to influence decisions. In this regard, the delay of the financial report may reduce its relevance in decision-making. For example, information from a weather forecast is only relevant if it is given prior to the date it concerns. After that, it can only be used to confirm if the forecast was reliable but it has lost most of its relevance for decision-making. In literature, the meaning of timeliness is commonly interpreted slightly different, and it is related to timely loss recognition. More timely loss recognition means more timely disclosure of losses and thus a more relevant information.

Another aspect of relevance is predictability. The IASB and the FASB Frameworks establish the notion of predictability referring to the predictive ability of the information. The predictability of earnings in this case is described as the relation of current and last year earnings to next years earnings. Hence, if the relation between current and next year earnings increases, then the predictive ability of the earnings' figures also increase. Information is reliable if it faithfully represents events and transactions (there are no material errors or bias). Reliability is described by the FASB as the "extent to which the accounting description or measurement is verifiable and representationally faithful". According to IASB, reliability adheres to information when it is free from material error and bias and it faithfully represents that which it either purports to represent or could reasonably be expected to represent.

The reliability characteristic consists of multiple elements: faithful representation, substance over form, neutrality, prudence, and completeness. Most important aspects in discussing reliability are representational faithfulness and neutrality. Information must faithfully represent the transactions and other events it either purports to represent or could reasonably be expected to represent, so that the information reflects the transactions and events that have happened or are expected to happen. Substance over form means that the information must reflect the economic transactions in place of the legal form of the contract. The information must also be and neutral to the decision of the user because bias might influence the decisions of users. Neutrality means that the information is free of bias in order to be reliable. The Frameworks of both IASB and FASB underline the neutrality of reported figures as an aspect supporting the reliability of the information. In order to measure this neutrality it is possible to use EM instead of a direct measure of neutrality. Logically, EM affects the earnings' neutrality as earnings that are managed contain a bias induced by the management.

4.3 Accounting Standards and Earnings Quality

The notion that different Accounting Standards are related to different degrees of EQ is evidenced in previous studies. This was marked by Ewert and Wagenhofer (2010) who found out that high-quality Accounting Standards decrease EM and increase reporting quality. By systematically modeling the effects of compelling Accounting Standards, Ewert and Wagenhofer (2010) concluded that high EQ can be achieved by applying strict Accounting Standards that both limit the number of accounting choices and prescribe clearer rules. In particular, the results confirm that tight Accounting Standards reduce EM and increase EQ (measured by the variability of reported earnings and the association between reported earnings and market price reactions). As every accounting choice has its costs and these costs increase with the frequency accounting choice is exercised, EM is expected to be more widely spread under lax regimes that allow sufficient discretion for making judgments.

Companies use earnings as a prime means to disseminate firm-specific information to their external users as they are a good indicator of future cash flows.[6] Earnings are considered to be the main source of information in capital markets (Schipper & Vincent, 2003) as they are more informative about a firm's economic performance than cash flows. Hence, earnings convey information of great significance about a company's value and the issue of EQ is of countless interest for financial market participants—particularly for investors and analysts—for better assessing performance and making correct investment decisions (Gaio & Raposo, 2011). Financial analysts use earnings for making forecasts about the securities' future outcomes. In addition, institutional investors and corporate boards are interested in earnings to value the quality of management as well as the overall firm's performance (Lev, 2003).

[6] In this regard, just in 1976 the FASB (1976) stated that: "The primary focus of financial reporting is information about an enterprise's performance provided by measures of earnings and its components. Investors, creditors and others who are concerned with assessing the prospects for enterprise net cash inflows are especially interested in that information. Their interest is an enterprise's future cash flows and its ability to generate favorable cash flows leads primarily to an interest in information about its earnings".

Accounting amounts that better reflect a firm's underlying economics, either resulting from principles-based standards or required accounting measurements, can increase accounting quality. These two sources of higher accounting quality limit opportunistic discretion by managers and they increase the extent to which the accounting amounts mirror a firm's underlying economics. In this regard, we believe that Accounting Standards limiting opportunistic discretion bring about accounting earnings that are more reflective of a firm's underlying economics and, consequently, that are of higher quality. Financial statements are prepared according to Generally Accepted Accounting Principles (GAAPs) that provide alternatives of treatments for the measurement of financial transactions. If the preparer (management) can choose among alternative accounting methodologies, the flexibility in selecting a method from a set of accounting policies opens up the possibility of opportunistic behavior. This leads to EM (Scott, 2012) that is one dimension of accounting quality. When firms perform EM, the quality of accounting information in financial reporting will be lower compared to those firms not managing their earnings.

EM is the choice of certain accounting policies that a manager makes to achieve some specific reported earnings objective. With regards to freedom in choosing accounting policies, there are two categories of accounting policies. The first is the choice of accounting policies per se, and the second is discretionary accruals. In the second category are included: provisions for credit losses, warranty costs, inventory values, and timing and amounts of low-persistence items such as write-offs. Management has always the responsibility for the selection and the application of accounting principles, as well as the underlying estimates and judgments used in applying such principles. It is important to recognize that the quality of accounting principles is not the same as the quality of earnings, but the two are inherently linked in that the judgments used in selecting and applying such principles directly impact the quality of earnings. Hence, management is ultimately responsible for the quality of earnings.

In particular, three sets of decisions within the context of Accounting Standards might affect EQ:

1. decisions made by Standard Setters;
2. management's decisions related to which accounting methods should they choose from a set of alternatives;

3. judgments and estimates made by managers in order to implement these accounting methods.

4.3.1 IAS/IFRSs and Earnings Quality

One of the IASB's main objectives is the development of a single set of high quality, understandable, enforceable, and globally accepted Accounting Standards. As a requirement, IAS/IFRSs poses that the information of financial reporting (and specifically of financial statements) must be of high quality, transparent, and comparable. Thus, this set of Accounting Standards contribute to improve the quality of annual reports (i.e., accounting quality) and further to help capital market participants and other users to make appropriate economic decisions (Armstrong et al., 2010). With this aim, the IASB have issued principles-based standards and have taken steps both to remove allowable accounting alternatives and to require accounting measurements that better reflect a firm's economic position and performance. Accounting quality could increase if these Standard Setters' actions limit management's opportunistic discretion in determining accounting amounts.

Generally, IAS/IFRSs are considered to be a high-quality set of Accounting Standards, which contributes to the improvement of the annual reports' quality. However, the IAS/IFRSs are principles-based standards as the accountants need to use considerable professional judgment to adapt general principles to specific situations (Ball, 2006). Hence, the quality of annual reports is still a matter of subjective determination.

The last updated IAS/IFRSs have reduced the number of allowed alternative accounting treatments and have required accounting measurements and disclosure to better reflect an entity's underlying financial position and performance in the financial reporting. The disclosure of high-quality accounting information in IAS/IFRSs-based financial statements assists investors in making informed and unbiased judgments because it involves less information asymmetry.

The goal is the protection of investors and the restoration of confidence in financial markets, especially after the outbreak of big financial scandals around the world and the increase of competitiveness of the European Union (EU)'s economy, globally. Also, the intention of European Commission in endorsing IAS/IFRSs was the improvement of the accounting quality of all the financial statements of companies operating in the Member States of the EU. We would expect financial reporting under IAS/IFRSs to be increasingly value relevant and reliable although the mere adoption of IAS/IFRSs is not sufficient to guarantee a better quality of accounting information. Legal and political systems also affect accounting quality directly, through enforcement of Accounting Standards and litigation against managers and auditors. This enforcement role of legal systems is especially important when the accounting quality following the adoption of IAS/IFRSs is considered. The legal system is therefore very important in determining accounting quality under situations that are not prescribed under IAS/IFRSs and that need an interpretation of the principles. In countries with strong shareholders' protection, we suppose that the interpretation leans toward a fair presentation of information to shareholders. In countries with strong creditors' protection, instead, we assume that the interpretation satisfies contracting demands of banks, i.e., conservative approaches to record assets and aggressive approaches to record liabilities. In line with these perspectives, two main sub-objectives of information usefulness are identified, i.e., the information must be contracting relevant and valuation relevant (Christensen, Feltham, & Sabac, 2005). These two objectives of informational usefulness can be in conflict with each other. The difference between the contracting perspective (also named stewardship) and the valuation perspective is that the stewardship looks more at the interest of creditors, while the valuation perspective looks at the ability of information to determine the value of the firms, thus looking more at the interest of investors. The objective of stewardship can thus result in a more conservative reporting and in a preference of HCA over current value accounting.[7]

[7] Acccording to the current value accounting, assets and liabilities are measured at the current value at which they could be sold or settled as of the current date. This accounting method varies from the historically based method because assets and liabilities are recorded at the amounts at which they were originally acquired or incurred (conservative approach). Compared to historically based method, current value accounting is that it provides information to the readers of a company's financial statements that most closely relates to current business conditions.

4.4 The Effects of IAS/IFRSs Adoption on Earnings Quality

There have been many studies exploring the influence of IAS/IFRSs on EQ but the empirical results are mixed and do not reach any definitive conclusions about this topic. Some studies (Ismail, Kamarudin, van Zijl, & Dunstan, 2013; Lin, Hua, Lin, & Lee, 2012; Liu, Yao, Hu, & Liu, 2011) showed that IAS/IFRSs' adoption is associated with high quality of reported earnings and lower earnings smoothing (Ozili & Outa, 2019). Similarly, Zeghal, Chtourou, and Fourati (2012) stated that there has been some improvement in accounting quality after the IAS/IFRSs' adoption and in particular there has been an increase in the accounting-based attributes. Using a sample based on 1574 in European countries between 2001 and 2008, Zeghal et al. (2012) demonstrated that mandatory adopters show less EM, high quality of accounting accruals, and less loss avoidance. Timeliness, conservatism, and value relevance are not improved. Houqe, Van Zijl, Dunstan, and Karim (2012), using a sample of 24,034 firm-years in 16 EU countries, reported similar results. A recent research paper (Kwon, Na, & Park, 2019) examined the effect of Korea's mandatory adoption of IFRSs on EQ. The findings provided evidence of improved EQ by documenting smaller real EM, higher accrual quality, stronger earnings persistence, an increase in the value relevance of earnings, more accurate analysts' earnings forecasts.

On the contrary, other studies found that IAS/IFRSs do not improve reporting quality of companies (Ames, 2013; Cameran, Campa, & Pettinicchio, 2014; Doukakis, 2014; Liu & Sun, 2015). For example, Ahmed, Neel, and Wang (2013) found that mandatory IAS/IFRSs' adoption leads to greater income smoothing, larger accounting accruals, and less timely loss recognition[8] of economic losses, which means a deterioration in EQ.

In line with the majority of previous evidence about the extent of EQ associated with various Accounting Standards, it could be assumed that the adoption of IAS/IFRSs has some impacts on the quality of earnings. Companies applying IAS/IFRSs exhibit higher accounting quality in terms of: less management of earnings toward a target, less income smoothing, less loss avoidance, more value relevance, more timely recognition of losses and higher association of accounting information

[8] Our metric for timely loss recognition is the frequency of large negative net income.

with share prices and returns. This is because the implementation of IAS/IFRSs may promote the timely recognition of economic losses through the expanding measurement of Fair Value and would also make accounting figures informative. Due to greater disclosure requirements and greater emphasis on the use of Fair Value in IAS/IFRSs, EQ has a significant positive association with the adoption of this set of Standards according to prior literature (Houqe et al., 2012; Ismail et al., 2013; Kwon et al., 2019). From this point of view, the implementation of IAS/IFRSs would seem to increase the value relevance of accounting information (Arum, 2013; Liu et al., 2011; Okafor & Warsame, 2016) since FV implies the timely loss recognition of profit and loss in financial reporting.

The following two key features of IAS/IFRSs can be highlighted on EQ:

(1) IAS/IFRSs are principles-based Standards as they are basic principles and do not set detailed rules. In the accounting process, it is necessary to make judgments according to individual circumstances and economic events; (2) the use of Fair Value measurement. In particular, IAS/IFRSs require a more extensive use of FVA which could result in an improved ability of accounting numbers to capture the underlying economics on a timelier basis. Firms that adopt IAS/IFRSs are less likely to engage in earnings smoothing and are more likely to recognize losses in a proper manner. Finally, by enhancing the comparability of financial statements across countries, IAS/IFRSs potentially reduce the costs of processing and interpreting accounting information. Thus, they could enhance external monitoring of firms' accounting choices leading to improvements in accounting quality.

Based on the aforementioned characteristics, there are however conflicting but plausible arguments regarding whether or not the adoption of IAS/IFRSs specifically improves EQ (Sun, Cahan, & Emanuel, 2011). On one hand, the opportunity of Fair Value measurement to disclose the present value of assets and liabilities could improve EQ and provide useful information for investors' decision-making. On the other hand, principles-based Accounting Standards may increase managerial behaviors to manage earnings because Fair Value measurement may increase managers' flexibility with regard to the calculation of current values (e.g., Fair Value Accounting). For example, FVA permits companies to increase or decrease the value of assets and liabilities in the financial statements in order to reflect the changes in the market prices of the assets. Moreover, managers may engage in EM in order to communicate private information; in this case, an increase in EM could have a positive effect on EQ. Such features of EM could make the economic consequence of IAS/IFRSs adoption complicated.

Although the intent of the IASB in updating IAS/IFRSs was to better reflect an entity's underlying financial position and performance in the financial reporting, just the practical use of IAS/IFRSs may increase managerial discretionary behaviors and decrease the informativeness of accounting information through widely used Fair Value measurement under certain circumstances (i.e., the Level 3 measurement within the Fair Value hierarchy).[9] Within the accounting regime of Fair Value, the degree of managerial discretion in its calculation plays some role in determining the financial reporting quality (Kvaal & Nobes, 2012; Menicucci, 2015). When Fair Values are estimated using valuation models, managers can influence the measurements through their choices of the parameters, thus opening the doors to greater EM. Managers can exploit flexibility within the Level 3 Fair Value measurement to pursue their own reporting interests. Especially privately held firms (that have more concentrated ownership and major capital providers) often have insider access to corporate information so that earnings would not have to be as informative about the true economic performance. Moreover, management's bonuses might be earnings-based. Under this perspective, although shareholders have a clear interest in attaining non-manipulated numbers, executive compensation might represent relevant incentives for managers to manipulate earnings.

Accounting Standards are just one of many institutional features in a country that influence firms' and managers' reporting incentives, actual reporting and disclosure outcomes. In other words, adopting a set of Accounting Standards that is viewed as of high quality does not necessarily improve EQ. Rather, it may be important to establish institutional environments that enforce the Accounting Standards' function appropriately. Besides Accounting Standards, EQ is influenced by firm and country-level investor protection (Houqe et al., 2012; Leuz et al., 2003). EQ increases for mandatory IAS/IFRSs' adoption where a country's investor protection system

[9] For a close examination, see Chapter 5.

offers stronger protection for its investors (Houqe et al., 2012). The improvement of EQ mainly depends on two factors: high quality of Accounting Standards and a country's overall investor protection (Soderstrom & Sun, 2007). In countries with strong investor protection there is a larger financial transparency and less EM—all of which could be interpreted as indicators of higher accounting quality (Bhattacharya, Desai, & Venkataraman, 2013; Bushman, Piotroski, & Smith, 2004). Strong country-level investor protection increases high-quality accounting information and then the interface of these two variables positively affects economic growth. Hence, in countries with strong investor protection there is a threatening relationship between accounting earnings and actual economic events.

Given the emphasis on the use of Fair Value and the greater disclosure requirements prescribed by IAS/IFRSs (Ru & Baljit, 2018), we believe that there would be some impacts of the adoption of these Standards on the quality of earnings reported by companies. EQ is determined by the relevance of underlying financial performance to the decisions and the ability of the accounting system to measure this performance (Dechow, Ge, & Schrand, 2010). EQ depends both on accounting methods and judgments and on the interaction between companies' real activity and accounting policies; this implies that managers using these combined effects can manage earnings (Kothari, Mizik, & Roychowdhury, 2016). Finally, when earnings conform to the spirit and the rules of Generally Accepted Accounting Principles (GAAPs), they are of high quality in the eyes of regulators. Earnings should be free from fraud and show a true and fair view of a company's financial performance regardless of Accounting Standards. However, Accounting Standard Setters are also concerned with the effectiveness of the Standards they have promulgated. By focusing on the usefulness of earnings numbers to financial statement users, Standard Setters can evaluate as high the quality of earnings resulting from a particular set of Accounting Standards. In contrast, EQ means more than just meeting the requirements of the Accounting Standards and we do not agree with the assumption that if Accounting Standards are met, financial statements provide a fair view of earnings and financial position.

To examine the impact of IAS/IFRSs' adoption on the quality of reported earnings, we focus on two attributes of high quality of earnings

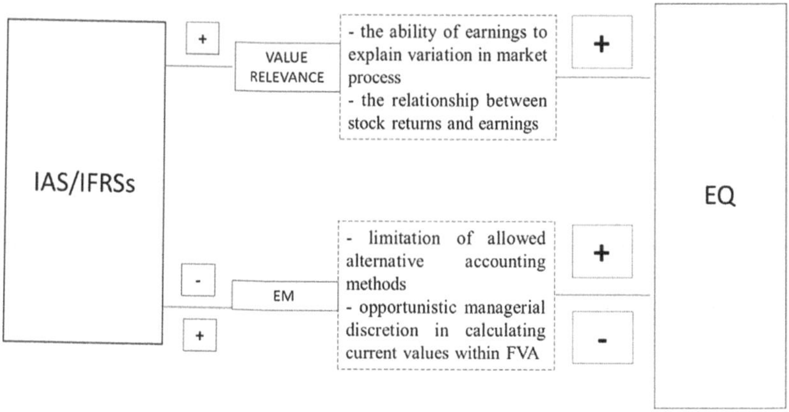

Fig. 4.1 IAS/IFRSs and EQ

in terms of lower level of EM practices[10] and higher value relevance[11] of earnings numbers. To this perspective, there are two approaches. The first is that EQ is inversely related to the amount of judgment and forecasting that the preparers of financial reports require. That is, when the possibility that reported numbers must be estimated by management increases— as part of the implementation of Reporting Standards—, then quality decreases. The second approach is that quality is inversely related to the extent accountants' estimations and forecasts get results other than those standards' target.

The following conceptual framework (Fig. 4.1) is developed to provide a basis for a comprehensive and perceptive discernment of the IAS/IFRSs' impact on EQ. In the diagram, IAS/IFRSs and EQ are independent and dependent variables, respectively.

[10]Our metrics for EM are based on the variance of the change in net income, the ratio of the variance of the change in net income to the variance of the change in cash flows, the correlation between accruals and cash flows, and the frequency of small positive net income. We interpret a higher variance of the change in net income, higher ratio of the variances of the change in net income and change in cash flows, less negative correlation between accruals and cash flows, and lower frequency of small positive net income as evidence of less EM.

[11]Our metrics for value relevance are the explanatory powers of net income and equity book value for prices, and stock return for earnings. We interpret higher explanatory power as evidence of more value relevance.

Accounting amounts resulting from the application of IAS/IFRSs are of higher quality than those resulting from the application of domestic Standards. Specifically, the adoption of IAS/IFRSs impacts on the extent of EM (Capkun, Collins, & Jeanjean, 2016) and on reported earnings' value relevance. These conclusions concerning IAS/IFRSs and EQ focused on the endorsement of FVA as a measurement base within this set of Accounting Standards. We expect that FVA results in a better ability of earnings to explain variation in market process with a high relationship between stock returns and earnings. Hence, the application of IAS/IFRSs is positively associated with EQ in terms of financial reporting's value relevance, information content and decision usefulness (Devalle, Onali, & Magarini, 2010).

Turning to EM, the effect of IAS/IFRSs on EQ is twofold. On one hand, the IAS/IFRSs are high-quality Standards being equipped with limitation of alternative accounting methods. We maintain that the IAS Standards that went into effect in 2005 provided greater flexibility of accounting choices because of vague criteria and subjective estimates. This large flexibility coupled with the lack of clear guidance on how to implement these Standards had led to greater EM (smoothing). Specifically, many of the first IAS/IFRS Standards have been broadly criticized for the absence of implementation guidance and for permitting great discretionary in application. Over the time, the revised Standards have reduced the number of allowed alternative accounting choices (Capkun et al., 2016) and, more recently, the IASB has provided greater implementation guidance through a series of interpretations by International Financial Reporting Interpretations Committee (IFRIC). It has also tried to promote greater consistency in earnings' measurement through a number of joint projects with the FASB and to endorse amendments to IAS/IFRS Standards (most notably the issue of IFRS 9 on revenue recognition and accounting of financial instruments).[12]

On the other hand, however, the opportunity of FVA increase managerial behaviors to manage earnings under certain circumstances because Fair Value measurement may amplify managers' discretion in measuring the current values of assets and liabilities (i.e., Level 3 valuation techniques based on subjective inputs and assumptions of managers). In this case, the inherent flexibility in Fair Value measurement allowed by IFRS

[12] Cfr. IFRS 9—*Financial Instruments*.

9 could provide greater opportunity for managers to manipulate earnings and greater potential for abuse through discretion, thereby decreasing EQ. Managers may smooth income using their discretion in estimating unobservable inputs within FVA, so that the smoother income pattern fails to reflect the true underlying risks. Consequently, IAS/IFRSs' adoption can result in more accounting manipulation and thus in lower EQ to some extent.

Bibliography

Ahmed, A. S., Neel, M., & Wang, D. (2013). Does mandatory adoption of IFRS improve accounting quality? Preliminary evidence. *Contemporary Accounting Research, 30*(4), 1344–1372.

Ames, D. (2013). IFRS adoption and accounting quality: The case of South Africa. *Journal of Applied Economics and Business Research, 3*(3), 154–165.

Armstrong, C. S., Barth, M. E., Jagolinzer, A. D., & Riedl, E. J. (2010). Market reaction to the adoption of IFRS in Europe. *The Accounting Review, 85*(1), 31–61.

Armstrong, C. S., Core, J. E., Taylore, D. J., & Verrecchia, R. E. (2011). When does information asymmetry affect the cost of capital? *Journal of Accounting Research, 49*(1), 1–40.

Arum, E. (2013). Implementation of International Financial Reporting Standards (IFRS) and the quality of financial statement information in Indonesia. *Research Journal of Finance and Accounting, 4*(19), 200–210.

Ball, R. (2006). International Financial Reporting Standards (IFRS): Pros and cons for investors. *Accounting and Business Research, 36*(s-1), 5–27.

Barth, M. E., Landsman, W. R., & Lang, M. H. (2008). International accounting standards and accounting quality. *Journal of Accounting Research, 46*(3), 467–498.

Bhattacharya, N., Desai, H., & Venkataraman, K. (2013). Does earnings quality affect information asymmetry? Evidence from trading costs. *Contenporary Accounting Research, 30*(2), 482–516.

Botosan, C. (2004). Discussion of a framework for the analysis of risk communication. *The International Journal of Accounting, 39*(3), 289–295.

Brown, S., & Hillegeist, S. (2007). How disclosure quality affects the level of information asymmetry. *Review of Accounting Studies, 12*(2–3), 443–477.

Burgstahler, D. C., Hail, L., & Leuz, C. (2006). The importance of reporting incentives: Earnings management in European private and public firms. *The Accounting Review, 81*(5), 983–1016.

Bushman, R. M., Piotroski, P. D., & Smith, A. J. (2004). What determines corporate transparency? *Journal of Accounting Research, 42*(2), 207–252.

Bushman, R. M., & Smith, A. J. (2003). Transparency, financial accounting information, and corporate governance. *Economic Policy Review, 9*(1), 65–87.

Cameran, M., Campa, D., & Pettinicchio, A. (2014). IFRS adoption among private companies: Impact on earnings quality. *Journal of Accounting, Auditing & Finance, 29*(3), 278–305.

Capkun, V., Collins, D., & Jeanjean, T. (2016). The effect of IAS/IFRS adoption on earnings management (smoothing): A closer look at competing explanations. *Journal of Accounting and Public Policy, 35*, 352–394.

Christensen, P. O., Feltham, G. A., & Sabac, F. (2005). A contracting perspective on earnings quality. *Journal of Accounting and Economics, 39*(2), 265–294.

Cohen, J. R., Krishnamoorthy, G., & Wright, A. (2004). The corporate governance mosaic and financial reporting quality. *Journal of Accounting Literature, 23*(1), 87–152.

Cormier, D., & Magnan, M. L. (2016). The advent of IFRS in Canada: Incidence on value relevance. *Journal of International Accounting Research, 15*(3), 113–130.

Daske, H., & Gebhardt, G. (2006). International financial reporting standards and experts' perceptions of disclosure quality. *Abacus, 42*(3–4), 461–498.

Daske, H., Hail, L., Leuz, C., & Verdi, R. S. (2008). Mandatory IFRS reporting around the world: Early evidence on the economic consequences. *Journal of Accounting Research, 46*(5), 1085–1142.

Dechow, P. M., & Dichev, I. D. (2002). The quality of accruals and earnings: The role of accrual estimation errors. *The Accounting Review, 77*(Suppl.), 35–59.

Dechow, P. M., Ge, W., & Schrand, C. (2010). Understanding earnings quality: A review of the proxies, their determinants and their consequences. *Journal of Accounting and Economics, 50*(2–3), 344–401.

Devalle, A., Onali, E., & Magarini, R. (2010). Assessing the value relevance of accounting data after the introduction of IFRS in Europe. *Journal of International Financial Management & Accounting, 21*(2), 85–119.

Doukakis, L. C. (2014). The effect of mandatory IFRS adoption on real and accrual-based earnings management activities. *Journal of Accounting and Public Policy, 33*(6), 551–572.

Dye, R. A., & Sunder, S. (2001). Why not allow FASB and IASB standards to compete in the U.S.? *Accounting Horizons, 15*(3), 257–271.

Ewert, R., & Wagenhofer, A. (2010). *Earnings quality metrics and what they measure* (Working Paper), University of Graz, Austria, full text available at http://dx.doi.org/10.1561/1400000025.

FASB. (1976, December). *Tentative conclusions objectives of financial statements of business enterprises.*

Gaio, C., & Raposo, C. C. (2011). Earnings quality and firm valuation: International evidence. *Accounting & Finance, 51*(2), 467–499.

Houqe, M. N., Van Zijl, T., Dunstan, K., & Karim, A. K. (2012). The effect of IFRS adoption and investor protection on earnings quality around the world. *The International Journal of Accounting, 47*(3), 333–355.

Hribar, P., Kravet, T., & Wilson, R. (2014). A new measure of accounting quality. *Review of Accounting Studies, 19*(1), 506–538.

Iatridis, G. (2011). Accounting disclosures, accounting quality and conditional and unconditional conservatism. *International Review of Financial Analysis, 20*(2), 88–102.

IASB. (2010). *Conceptual framework for financial reporting* (Conceptual Framework).

IASB. (2018). *Conceptual framework for financial reporting* (Conceptual Framework).

Ismail, W. A., Kamarudin, K. A., van Zijl, T., & Dunstan, K. (2013). Earnings quality and the adoption of IFRS-based accounting standards: Evidence from an emerging market. *Asian Review of Accounting, 21*(1), 53–73.

Kothari, S. P., Leone, A. J., & Charles, C. E. (2005). Performance matched discretionary accrual measures. *Journal of Accounting and Economics, 39*(1), 163–197.

Kothari, S. P., Mizik, N., & Roychowdhury, S. (2016). Managing for the moment: The role of earnings management via real activities versus accruals in SEO valuation. *The Accounting Review, 91*(2), 559–586.

Kvaal, E., & Nobes, C. (2012). IFRS policy changes and the continuation of national patterns of IFRS practice. *European Accounting Review, 21*(2), 343–371.

Kwon, S. Y., Na, K., & Park, J. (2019). The economic effects of IFRS adoption in Korea, Asia-Pacific. *Journal of Accounting and Economics, 26*(4), 321–361.

Lambert, R. A., Leuz, C., & Verrecchia, R. E. (2007). Accounting information, disclosure, and the cost of capital. *Journal of Accounting Research, 45*(2), 385–420.

Lambert, R. A., Leuz, C., & Verrecchia, R. E. (2012). Information asymmetry, information precision, and the cost of capital. *Review of Finance, 16*(1), 1–29.

Lang, M., Raedy, J. S., & Wilson, W. (2006). Earnings management and cross listing: Are reconciled earnings comparable to US earnings? *Journal of Accounting and Economics, 42*(1–2), 255–283.

Lang, M., Ready, J. S., & Yetman, M. H. (2003). How representative are firms that are cross-listed in the United States? An analysis of accounting quality. *Journal of Accounting Research, 41*(2), 363–386.

Leuz, C., Nanda, D., & Wyscocki, P. D. (2003). Earnings management and investor protection: An international comparison. *Journal of Financial Economics, 69*(3), 505–527.

Leuz, C., & Verrecchia, R. E. (2000). The economic consequences of increased disclosure. *Journal of Accounting Research, 38*(Suppl.), 91–124.

Lev, B. (2003). Corporate earnings: Facts and fiction. *Journal of Economic Perspectives, 17*(2), 27–50.
Levitt, A. (1998). The importance of high quality accounting standards. *Accounting Horizons, 12*(1), 79–82.
Lin, C. C., Hua, C. Y., Lin, W. H., & Lee, W. C. (2012). IFRS adoption and financial reporting quality: Taiwan experience. *International Journal of Academic Research in Accounting, Finance and Management Sciences,* 2(4), 285–294.
Liu, C., & Sun, J. (2015). Did the mandatory adoption of IFRS affect the earnings quality of Canadian firms? *Accounting Perspectives, 14*(3), 250–275.
Liu, C., Yao, L. J., Hu, N., & Liu, L. (2011). The impact of IFRS on accounting quality in a regulated market: An empirical study of China. *Journal of Accounting, Auditing & Finance, 26*(4), 659–676.
Menicucci, E. (2015). *Fair value accounting: Key issues arising from the financial crisis.* London, UK: Palgrave Macmillan.
Nichols, D., & Wahlen, J. M. (2004). How do earnings numbers relate to stock returns? A review of classic accounting research with updated evidence. *Accounting Horizons, 18*(4), 263–286.
Okafor, O. N., & Warsame, M. A. H. (2016). IFRS and value relevance: Evidence based on Canadian adoption. *International Journal of Managerial Finance, 12*(2), 136–160.
Ozili, P., & Outa, E. (2019). Bank earnings smoothing during mandatory IFRS adoption in Nigeria. *African Journal of Economic and Management Studies, 10*(1), 32–47.
Penman, S. (2003). The quality of financial statements: Perspectives from the recent stock market bubble. *Accounting Horizons, 17*(1), 77–96.
Ribeiro, A., Shan, Y., & Taylor, S. (2019). Convergence of accounting standards and financial reporting externality: Evidence from mandatory IFRS adoption. *Abacus, 55*(1), 6–41.
Ronen, J., & Yaari, V. (2008). *Earnings management: Emerging insights in theory, practice and research.* New York: Springer.
Ru, G., & Baljit, S. (2018). Convergence of accounting standards and financial reporting externality: Evidence from mandatory IFRS adoption. *Accounting & Finance, 58*(3), 817–848.
Schipper, K., & Vincent, L. (2003). Earnings quality. *Accounting Horizons, 17*(s-1), 97–110.
Scott, W. R. (2012). *Financial accounting theory* (7th ed.). Toronto: Prentice-Hall.
Shaw, K. W. (2003). Corporate disclosure quality, earnings smoothing, and earnings' timeliness. *Journal of Business Research, 56*(12), 1043–1050.
Soderstrom, N. S., & Sun, K. J. (2007). IFRS adoption and accounting quality: A review. *European Accounting Review, 16*(4), 675–702.

Street, D. L., & Gray, S. J. (2002). Factors influencing the extent of corporate compliance with International Accounting Standards: Summary of a research monograph. *Journal of International Accounting, Auditing and Taxation, 11*(1), 51–76.

Sun, J., Cahan, S. F., & Emanuel, D. (2011). How would the mandatory adoption of IFRS affect the earnings quality of U.S. firms? Evidence from cross-listed firms in the U.S. *Accounting Horizons, 25*(4), 837–860.

Zeghal, D., Chtourou, S. M., & Fourati, Y. M. (2012). The effect of mandatory adoption of IFRS on earnings quality: Evidence from the European Union. *Journal of International Accounting Research, 11*(2), 1–25.

CHAPTER 5

Fair Value Accounting and Earnings Quality

Abstract The use of Fair Value in financial reporting has developed a current debate about the impact of an FVA-based reporting system on EQ. FVA leads to more current accounting information since it is a market-based measurement. Nevertheless, Fair Value is considered unreliable and often it is subject to managerial discretion, especially when markets are illiquid or distressed. High degree of subjectivity in estimation of Fair Value could allow management opportunities for the exercise of judgments and intentional bias which can decrease the quality of financial reporting. Management discretion can result in a higher EM and thus in a reduced amount of EQ. Managers engage in EM especially during periods of financial distress to mask the negative effects of the crisis (e.g., low profitability and bad financial performance).

Keywords Fair Value Accounting (FVA) · Earnings quality (EQ) · Earnings management (EM) · Financial reporting · Financial crisis

5.1 Introduction

The use of Fair Value in financial reporting has sparked an ongoing debate about the qualities of an FVA-based reporting system. In the last few years, a wide discussion emerged about the trade-off between relevance and reliability of accounting information, and, for the most part, this

E. Menicucci, *Earnings Quality*,
https://doi.org/10.1007/978-3-030-36798-5_5

debate has especially centered on the relevance versus the reliability of FVA. Motivated by the objectives of financial reporting stated by the Accounting Standard Setters (International Accounting Standard Board—IASB—and Financial Accounting Standard Board—FASB), we investigate whether the use of Fair Value in financial reports is related to EQ. Accounting academics have raised concerns about the impacts of FVA on EQ mainly by investigating the effects on volatility and predictability of future cash flows and earnings. Despite the many efforts made by the IASB and the FASB to amend Standards that can improve accounting quality, in recent years authors questioned the success of these sets of Accounting Standards in this regard. Moreover, in the context of the financial crisis and the contraction of credit that followed, a few studies have inspected the role of FVA in these circumstances (Bhat, Frankel, & Martin, 2011; Bowen, Khan, & Rajgopal, 2009; Khan, 2011; Laux & Leuz, 2009, 2010; Menicucci & Paolucci, 2016).

5.2 Fair Value Accounting and Financial Reporting

The main consequence of the adoption of IAS/IFRSs is the movement from HCA toward FVA that is expected to result in more relevant, timely, credible, and transparent financial statements.

5.2.1 *The Shift from Historical Cost Accounting to Fair Value Accounting*

The traditional way for valuing assets and liabilities is based on Historical Cost Model, i.e., assets and liabilities are carried at their past entry values, equal to the amount of consideration given or received at the time of the acquisition of assets or when the liabilities were incurred. The Historical Cost is considered to be reliable and verifiable, as it is based on actual transactions and free from bias. However, Historical Cost was also alleged to lack relevance for the decision-making process, as it does not reflect current market conditions. To cope with current market expectations, the Historical Cost paradigm is traditionally paired with prudence principle which allows adjustments in the value of assets and liabilities only for incorporating bad news. This paradigm eventually leads to understatements of assets and/or overstatements of liabilities and, accordingly, to bias. Differently, Fair Value[1] usually identifies with the market value, if there is a deep and liquid market for assets and liabilities. As an alternative, Fair Value is measured by estimating the value for which one could realize the asset (extinguish the liability) if the market value is unavailable. Hence, estimation of Fair Value creates opportunities for the exercise of management judgment and intentional bias which can decrease the quality of financial reporting (Hitz, 2007; Nissim, 2003). FVA allows for too many accounting alternatives that present a high amount of subjectivity, creating a path for opportunistic behaviors (Callao Gastón & Jarne, 2010).

The use of FVA has some advantages and disadvantages compared to HCA. The use of market values in FVA implies the account for potential income (not fully realized) in income statement as assets and liabilities are recognized at their market value even if they are not subject to purchase or sale. In this regard, Fair Value seems to increase transparency as far as it captures probable income accruing incorporating expected cash flows from assets and liabilities. By the use of market values for measuring different assets and liabilities, the amounts recognized in balance sheet are more relevant compared to the Historical Costs. When the value of assets and liabilities fluctuates much, Historical Costs become irrelevant over time while current values show the most relevant and up-to-date price. In this regard, FVA was implemented because in the balance sheets the values would be more informative and give earlier insights into the riskiness of the companies compared to HCA. If amounts fluctuate a lot from year to year, then the investor can see that the company is taking a lot of risk if the values of its assets and liabilities depend on the market conditions. This leads to more current accounting information for the investors that can ponder the riskiness of a business relying on balance sheets under Fair Value (Allen & Carletti, 2008). As the carrying

[1] IFRS 13—*Fair Value Measurement* defines Fair Value as "the price that would be received to sell an asset or paid to transfer a liability in an orderly transaction between market participants at the measurement date (an exit price)". Although Fair Value is becoming more and more important as a valuation model, it is not yet generalized for all assets and liabilities (i.e., full Fair Value model). Under both IAS/IFRSs and US GAAPs, there is a mixed valuation model including both Fair Value and Historical Cost, which continues to be applied together with the prudence principle in some circumstances. Fair Value measurements apply mainly for financial assets and liabilities, although there are Fair Value options allowed for non-financial items, such as revaluation models permitted for tangible assets and intangible fixed assets.

amounts in the balance sheet fluctuate a lot from year to year depending on market conditions for the most part, thus the values' changes will go through profit or loss leading to volatile earnings. In some situations (e.g., an illiquid market), the market price can be hard to determine and a valuation model must be used. The reluctance of companies to show which model and what assumptions they used reduces the comparability of the financial statements between companies. Because the model and the assumptions are sometimes unknown, the manager can manipulate the amounts more easily. In this perspective, FVA has some disadvantages, i.e., the possibility of manipulation by managers, the pro-cyclical effect, increased volatile accounting numbers, and the short-term orientation of financial reporting.

Anyway, the shift from HCA toward FVA in measurement paradigms is initiated by the presumed belief of higher quality and decision relevance of market-based measures than those of cost-based ones. In contrast, we believe that this assumption cannot be held in all circumstances, especially for financial reporting in an environment with inactive or inefficient markets. In this context, the lack of reliable market data (or even the lack of market data) requires the companies to use valuation techniques (i.e., mark to model) to estimate Fair Value more often than in an active market (Sŏdan, 2015). This could enable opportunistic EM and consequently could lower the quality of reported earnings. Moreover, FVA has a pro-cyclical effect. This means that assets (liabilities) are likely to be overstated (understated) during economic growth where assets (liabilities) are understated (overstated) during a recession. This leads earnings that are higher during an economic growth and lower during a recession. Since the revaluations do not always lead to realized gains and losses, the performance measures could be artificially volatile.

5.2.2 *The Informativeness of Fair Value*

The majority of previous studies on FVA investigated its informativeness for investors in capital markets. Evidence generally suggests that the implementation of FVA has actually increased the level of usefulness and value relevance of accounting information. The use of Fair Value enhances the relevance of the reported numbers compared to Historical Cost because it reflects market values and has more economical meaning than cost. Especially, researchers mostly agree that Fair Value—as it reflects market value—provides useful information regarding the amounts, timing, and uncertainty of future cash flows (Barth, 2008; Hitz, 2007; Landsman, 2007). The use of Fair Value estimates offers timely information about the changes in economic conditions and can serve as an early warning of adverse market conditions. However, when the determination of the Fair Value is not based on reliable observable inputs, its estimate is less relevant as the valuation parameters of Fair Value are not stable across time, i.e., they decrease during periods of economic turmoil due to greater illiquidity and information risk (Allen & Carletti, 2008). Regarding the usefulness of FVA, we believe that Fair Value is informative to investors, but the level of informativeness is affected by the amount of measurement error and source of the estimates (management or external appraisers).

The most critical issue of the Fair Value paradigm is an increase in relevance of accounting information as subsequent measurements of assets and liabilities at Fair Values (that can be estimated based on current market conditions) allow for the recognition of both unrealized gains and losses either in profit or loss (P&L) or as other comprehensive income (OCI). Market prices provide the most relevant and timely measures of assets and liabilities, and then Fair Values deliver the most current and complete estimations for the value of assets and obligations as well as information about the timing and riskiness of future cash flows. A high amount of reliability, verifiability, and lack of bias are attributable to FVA information since it is a market-based measurement. Nevertheless, when markets are illiquid or distressed, Fair Value is unreliable and often it is subject to managerial discretion. For some assets and liabilities, observable market transactions or other market information may not be available, and in such cases, an entity should rely on other valuation techniques. The IASB has established a Fair Value hierarchy[2] that classifies the inputs of different valuation techniques employed for Fair Value measurements into three levels. In other words, the Fair Value can be determined using three different approaches.

The first method consists in identifying Fair Value with quoted prices (unadjusted) in active markets[3] for identical assets or liabilities (mark to

[2] Cfr. IFRS 13—*Fair Value Measurement.*

[3] The classification of financial instruments within Level 1 is linked to the existence of two requirements. The first is the presence of an active market as defined in IFRS 13—*Fair Value Measurement.* IFRS 13 defines an active market as a market in which transactions for the asset or liability take place with sufficient frequency and volume to

market—Level 1). This is an easy and reliable way for multiple assets and liabilities. For example, prices of securities are usually determined using this way because stock markets are liquid and active markets. The price should then be determined by inputs (other than quoted prices included within Level 1) that are observable for the asset or liability, either directly (i.e., as prices) or indirectly (i.e., derived from prices) (mark to matrix—Level 2). The estimate of the Fair Value within Level 2 (as well as Level 3) requires the use of valuation techniques. If the valuation techniques are based on observable inputs that do not require adjustments (based on unobservable inputs), the financial instrument is classified in Level 2 (adjusted mark to market or mark to matrix). Finally, if the estimation within the Level 2 is not possible, the price should be determined by using a valuation model with assumptions that are based on internal estimates and calculations (mark to model—Level 3). Although in all cases Fair Value should be determined as an exit price at the measurement date from the perspective of a market participant (that holds the asset or owes the liability), in some cases inputs that are not based on observable market data (unobservable inputs) may also be used (mark to model) for recognizing the asset or the liability. Level 3 valuation techniques include subjective inputs and assumptions (such as a financial forecast developed using the entity's own data) with respect to those inputs. Hence, Level 1 uses unadjusted quoted market prices, while Level 2 and Level 3 Fair Value estimates use inputs and assumptions determined by managers. This hierarchy can provide timely information on how economic conditions may impact on value, but also allows significant management discretion in measurement and classification. According to IASB, the Fair Value hierarchy gives highest priority to quoted prices (unadjusted) in active markets for identical assets or liabilities (Level 1 inputs) and the lowest priority to unobservable inputs (Level 3 inputs). Following previous research, we use the amount of Fair Value estimated at Levels 2 and 3 in the Fair Value hierarchy (i.e., the discretionary Fair Value) to indicate the level of potential managerial discretion in Fair Value measurement (managerial

provide pricing. The concept of active market concerns the individual financial instrument being valued and not the market in which it is quoted. Therefore, the fact that a financial instrument is quoted on a regulated market is not, in itself, a sufficient condition for the instrument to be defined as quoted in an active market. The second requirement is represented by the term "unadjusted", i.e., the quote must not be adjusted.

discretion is difficult to measure). Managers are expected to disclose relatively more assets at Levels 2 and 3 to avoid directly recognizing losses in earnings when market conditions are expected to deteriorate. If greater managerial discretion in estimating Fair Value leads to a greater extent of EM, then earnings would become less reliable. The more Fair Value can be classified at Level 2 and Level 3, the more managerial discretion in determining Fair Value is exercisable. In turn, greater managerial discretion increases the opportunities to manage earnings, weakening earnings informativeness.

Hence, over the past years many criticisms have been moved to Fair Value and its reliability (King, 2008; Landsman, 2007; Ronen & Yaari, 2008). In particular, many authors revealed concerns about the hierarchy of inputs used and more generally about the degree of transparency in the valuation process when markets are illiquid. This mainly derives from the use of unobservable inputs and discretionary items that could allow opportunistic behavior by managers with the aim of achieving their bonus compensation goals and meeting investors' expectations. In this context, an extensive use of unobservable inputs and management manipulations in the estimation process could imply deceptive results (Benston, 2008). Additionally, the occurrence of value-irrelevant components of earnings turns to a decrease in their information content.

This condition seems to mainly depend on the extent of the use of unobservable inputs in the evaluation process as an intensive use of them could result in biased estimates (Pompili & Tutino, 2019a, b). Such a circumstance could give rise to: (1) a lower quality of accounting disclosure to stakeholders; (2) EM practices; and (3) information asymmetries influencing negatively the efficient investment allocations (Siekkinen, 2016; Song, Thomas, & Yi, 2010). FVA—specifically the Level 3—allows managers to use discretionary in estimates of unobservable inputs, even opportunistically (management manipulations). Managers turn to biased estimates of Fair Value in order to show the achievement of specific objectives in terms of performance and then to meet market expectations in this regard. When market values are not directly observable, estimates could be highly dependent on managers' choices and opportunistically manipulated by them within the estimation process. In this case, FVA could lead to information asymmetry (and eventually to moral hazard) because of the use of private information not clearly disclosed to stakeholders (Tutino & Pompili, 2019).

As a result, biased estimates could enhance information asymmetries and amplify EM that negatively influences EQ (Lo, 2008; Lobo & Zhou, 2001). In this regard, we consider the definition of Healy and Wahlen's (1999) according to which "earnings management occurs when managers use judgment in financial reporting and in structuring transactions to alter financial reports to either mislead some stakeholders about the underlying economic performance of the company or to influence contractual outcomes that depend on reported accounting numbers".

In literature, it is possible to find many kinds of research that analyze the relationship between management manipulation and FVA to understand if managers have possibilities and incentives to hold a such accounting behavior under the FVA approach. There is a link between the level of observability of inputs adopted for Fair Value estimation and management ability to influence accounting values. The hierarchy of Fair Value inputs also results in different investors' perceptions of reported value. In particular, a lower amount of inputs' observability is related to less reliable Fair Values and major investors' concerns about management estimation process (errors or manipulations). By observing the way the Fair Value is determined, it is clear that relevance seems more important than the reliability. Especially regarding the assets and liabilities for which there is not an active or liquid market, the price is determined in a way that is complex to verify. Companies are not willing to disclose which model and what assumptions they used, and due to this unwillingness, the Fair Value can be more easily manipulated by managers to show higher or lower earnings, depending on the situation.

5.2.3 *Fair Value Accounting and Earnings Volatility*

Within the context of FVA, previous empirical studies mainly investigated the relation between unrealized gains and losses from changes in Fair Values and future performance measures (operating cash flows or earnings). Higher volatility arises from the definition of Fair Value which refers to the present values of a series of expected future cash flows. Since Fair Value changes from year to year, the values recognized in the balance sheets would be driven by short-term fluctuations of the market that do not reflect the value of the fundamentals and the value at maturity of assets and liabilities. Fair Values are volatile because any subsequent adjustments in expectation of future cash flows automatically induce changes of Fair Values. In this regard, empirical studies almost totally proved that the move from HCA toward FVA leads to increased earnings volatility (Hodder, Hopkins, & Wahlen, 2006; Magnan, 2009; Plantin, Sapra, & Shin, 2008; Sun, Cahan, & Emanuel, 2011).

To the extent the volatility of Fair Values corresponds to the underlying economic volatility, FVA meets the objectives of financial reporting by providing information related to the uncertainty and timing of future cash flows. Besides, earnings persistence and predictive ability are often closely related to the amount of earnings volatility. Anyway, financial statements' volatility per se is not an indication of flawed financial reporting. On the contrary, providing information relating to the uncertainty and timing of future cash flows (inherent volatility) is a key indicator of a complete financial reporting. We can identify three possible sources of financial statements' volatility that are associated with Fair Value: inherent volatility, estimation error volatility, and mixed-measurement volatility (Barth, 2004). The first is actual underlying economic volatility that is mirrored by changes in the Fair Value of assets and liabilities. Inherent or economic volatility is not caused by the accounting process, but it is related to the characteristics of the assets and/or liabilities that are measured. The estimation error volatility refers to the volatility that is embedded in the reported Fair Value estimate due to the volatility of error with which the asset or liability is measured. Hence, the estimation error volatility results from imperfect measurements as it is forced by measurement error in estimates of Fair Values. Estimation error volatility should be smaller if Fair Value is determined based on the prices from active markets (mark to market) and should be larger if Fair Value is determined using estimation models and subjective assessments. Third, mixed-measurement volatility is an artificial source of volatility which derives from mixed-attribute reporting system where some assets and liabilities are measured at Historical Cost and others are measured at Fair Value.[4]

Fair Value tends to be more volatile than Historical Cost estimates because any change in the expectations relating to future cash flows results in a change in Fair Value estimates, even if they might be due to short-term market fluctuations. In this regard, the critics of FVA claim that Fair

[4] Estimation error volatility refers to the volatility induced in reported Fair Values due to the lack of well-specified estimation models. Mixed-measurement volatility arises because of the different measurement objectives used to measure and report assets and liabilities. Some assets and liabilities are measured at Historical Cost, some at lower of cost or a current value and others at Fair Value.

Values bear little association with future cash flows because the recognition of gains and losses is driven by short-term market movements rather than by an earned income or a loss incurred (Chisnall, 2001). Moreover, Fair Value estimates might embody volatility in excess of the underlying economic volatility because it is enhanced by estimation error volatility and mixed-measurement volatility.

5.3 Fair Value Accounting and Its Influence on Earnings Quality

The underlying assumption concerning the value relevance of FVA is its predictive ability of future cash flows and earnings. Therefore, the usefulness of Fair Value information can be directly examined by analyzing the insights in this regard. Under a full Fair Value-based accounting system, the balance sheet should provide complete information about the value of the firm's assets and obligations.[5] In this case, the income statement would report the changes in Fair Value as by the balance sheet. The earnings are influenced by FVA because subsequent measurements of assets and impairment testing lead to gains or losses that go straight to profit and loss statement. If a large part of the assets has to be measured subsequently at Fair Value, earnings might fluctuate and might be unreliable much depending on the market conditions.

When markets are liquid, Fair Values are reliable measures of assets and liabilities since the estimates represent the present value of expected future cash flows and their variations (e.g., unrealized gains and losses) should be reflected in changes in future performance. In this case, Fair Value measurements at Level 1 and Level 2 (designed for active markets) reflect the volatility of the active market and provide greater value relevance to financial statements' users than the Level 3 valuations (designed for products without an active market). Conversely, when markets are illiquid or inactive, Fair Value estimates are potentially unreliable due to the absence of quoted market prices and the inherent error in either the measurement technique or the inputs of it (Level 3 valuations). In other words, Fair Value measurements may be resulting from models that include basic

[5] Generally Accepted Accounting Principles (GAAPs) do not employ a full Fair Value-based accounting system. Rather, we have a mixed-attribute model under which certain items are reported at Fair Value and others are reported on a different measurement basis (e.g., amortized cost).

assumptions and valuation inputs (i.e., cash flow or income forecasts) that are discretionary. The increased subjectivity in estimating Fair Value may introduce possible alterations of the earnings and may affect the stakeholders' perception of risk.

Thus, bank managers may have some motivations for a misrepresentation of earnings (i.e., EM). This means that managers may smooth earnings to: (1) reduce earnings volatility, (2) signal lower risk to the market, (3) achieve stable compensations, and/or (4) manage the regulatory capital.

Accordingly, we investigate whether earnings which contain more Fair Value-based information are better predictors of future cash flows and future earnings than Historical Cost. Another alleged shortcoming of the Fair Value model is that it induces an increased volatility of earnings that can trigger share prices' volatility and increased forecast errors. When Fair Value is calculated through valuation techniques based on the entity's own assumptions and estimates, then FVA risks to being less reliable and less informative about future cash flows. Fair Value measurement suffers from unreliable estimates and managerial desires to avoid reporting mark to market losses. In this regard, further application of FVA would develop this discretionary behavior, so the value relevance of the accounting numbers would be reduced and the misleading behavior induced by the increased volatility would be increased. Nevertheless, as noted in Chapter 3, discretionary accounting choices either can be used to reveal private information about the firm or can be opportunistic and possibly misleading of the firm's economic performance. In the first case, we expect IAS/IFRSs-based earnings to be more reflective of firm's economic performance. In the second case, management discretion will result in a higher EM and thus in a reduced amount of EQ. Cautions against the adoption of full FVA are appropriate when managers are naturally inclined toward optimistic assessment of their business plans (Penman, 2007). Accounting's role as counterweight to assist equity investors in the firm valuation process is undermined when hypothetical Fair Value—based on optimistic managerial assumptions—is admitted into the accounting system.

Accordingly, the use of Fair Value concept may have different effects on EQ due to several aspects. Namely, as European companies rely on debt capital to a greater extent, the focus of financial reporting is less oriented toward investors' needs on capital markets because it is more set on creditors, suppliers, and other users. Also, it is likely that in such environment, active market prices for large portion of assets and liabilities are not available, so Fair Values are likely to be determined based on the model estimates (mark to model). Even though managers could use opportunities for discretion in order to convey private information to investors and consequently to improve EQ, we argue that managers are more likely to behave opportunistically in an environment with frail shareholders' protection (Hung, 2000). Even without the intentional misrepresentation by managers, the more subjective nature of Level 3 Fair Value estimates potentially leads to greater information asymmetry and therefore to greater estimation error. From this point of view and taken the mentioned aspects all together, we believe that higher exposure to FVA is negatively related to EQ.

5.4 The Effect of Fair Value Accounting on Earnings Response Coefficient (ERC)

As discussed above, if a large part of assets and liabilities are measured subsequently at Fair Value, earnings might fluctuate much depending on the market conditions. The earnings are influenced by FVA because subsequent measurements at Fair Values impact on profit and loss account.

Since the effect of Fair Value on the earnings-return relation is unknown, it is interesting to investigate if FVA has an effect on the earnings response coefficient (ERC). Little research has examined this relationship yet, and prior research mostly focused on one specific element of this relation. The importance of ERC research arises mainly from the need to enhance confidence of stakeholders in accounting information announcements, especially the equity investors, enabling them to make informed stock decisions. The ERC measures the informativeness of earnings in relation to the stock return as it is a measure of the relation between stock returns and earnings around the time the earnings are announced. In other words, ERC is the estimated relationship between equity returns and the unexpected portion of companies' earnings announcements.[6] Hence, ERC measures how much new information the earnings contain, and this new information is measured by examining the influence on the stock return around the announcement. The ERC

[6] The earnings response coefficient (ERC) is the stock market reaction (the change in stock price) for one unit of unexpected earnings.

has been used in prior research (Donnelly, 2002; Hasanzade, Darabi, & Mahfoozi, 2013) to show the effect of accounting changes on how the earnings (including the changes) relate to and influence the returns. Hence, accounting changes affect earnings and then the ERC measures if these changes are reflected in the stock returns. Since Fair Value is claimed to be more value relevant and more informative than Historical Cost, we examine if the ERC modifies by the use of FVA. To inspect the reliability and relevance of earnings, we inspect the informativeness of earnings as reflected in investor's response to earnings announcements.

We expect that the ERC should be higher when Fair Value is argued to be more informative because of the frequent price fluctuations and price adjustments. The ability of FVA to predict future income realization is an important value-relevant attribute that strengthens the relationship between Fair Value information and stock prices despite the low persistence of changes in Fair Values. A higher ERC shows that the returns are more dependent on earnings and the earnings are more informative since the share price reacts more deeply to earnings.

The Level 1 estimation of Fair Value increases relevance of the financial statements; Fair Value reduces the uncertainty for investors in this case, and this should increase the ERC. On the contrary, Fair Value increases uncertainty about the carrying amounts of Level 2 and Level 3 assets. The uncertainty rises because some estimations of Fair Values are based on models and assumptions that are unknown to the investors. If the amounts cannot be verified, the reliability of the financial statements decreases as the estimates could be manipulated by managers to influence the figures in the financial statements. Earnings are influenced by the use of Fair Values, and thus, FVA influences the ERC either way.

FVA affects the ERC because it can artificially increase the volatility of earnings. In estimating Fair Value, managers may smooth income using their discretion based on unobservable inputs. It is interesting to see the effect of the artificial volatility (that fails to reflect true underlying risks) because the ERC might move along with the earnings changes and might be more volatile also. Concerning the relationship between earnings volatility and stock price volatility, the ERC could be lower since the earnings are not likely to persist in the future. Most volatile earnings are transitory and are not realized yet within FVA. The pro-cyclical effect of FVA leads to higher earnings during economic upturn and lower earnings during a recession also influencing ERC. If we accept that losses lower the informativeness of earnings, it could be argued that earnings incorporating Fair Value losses lead to lower ERC. If the proportion of the losses is largely due to Fair Value changes, the informativeness of earnings decreases or it is not affected because the expectations of future cash flows are not modified. Looking at the cash flows, investors might recognize that these cash flows haven't changed much in comparison with earnings, and therefore, the stock price might not have changed much.

5.5 The Impact of Fair Value Accounting on Earnings Quality During a Financial Crisis

The 2008 financial crisis has questioned the FVA as one of the factors that could have worsened its severity (Barth & Landsman, 2010; Laux & Leuz, 2009, 2010). Although accounting and banking do not consider FVA as the guilty of the crisis, they cannot point out it as a simple messenger that is now being shot (Bonaci, Matis, & Strouhal, 2010; Menicucci, 2015; Veron, 2008; Whittington, 2008) because it is rather a measurement system that produces economic effects on its own. In particular, Fair Value is considered a possible driver of the banking crisis and the credit crunch. Namely, critics have faulted FVA for intensifying the financial collapse, also triggering a falling prices' circle and thereby increasing the overall risk in the financial system (Khan, 2011). Highlighting the subject for banks, Fair Value has significant implications for the banking industry where financial instruments and loan loss provisions are recognized at FVA. Fair Value adjustments are volatile and can quickly undermine earnings and the equity cushion especially in banks' balance sheets.

With regard to the shortcomings of FVA, the main subject lies in the trade-off between relevance and reliability. Critics of FVA believe that Fair Values may be less relevant and/or reliable during periods of economic distress, such as the 2008 financial crisis when markets were less liquid and Fair Values were difficult to determine. Assets and liabilities measured at Fair Value reflect the current market conditions, and in this respect, FVA increases the transparency of financial reporting and encourages prompt corrective actions. However, there are legitimate concerns about mark to market accounting in times of financial crisis as it may cause market reactions over the short term. In this perspective, the impact of economic cycles on the predictive ability of Fair Value information in recognizing earnings can be very substantial from an accounting point of view. Since FVA is pro-cyclical, it amplifies the crisis in an economic downturn and feeds the growth in an economic upturn.

Critics contend that the Fair Value and the immediate recognition of losses when the market takes an extra downturn lead to an incorrect working pricing mechanism. As a consequence of amplified losses and a big capital gap, financial institutions have to sell assets for respecting capital requirements. Then, the timely reaction to the excess write-down leads to large losses and even lower prices. Liquidity problems also induce to lending at a higher interest rate. The large write-downs furthermore increase uncertainty for investors about the Level 3 financial assets and about the pricing methods that are used by companies to estimate these assets. Additionally, asset-backed securities come up from Level 1 to Level 3 assets because they become illiquid (as in a credit crisis), and hence, these securities have to be measured at discounted prices in the market. During the growth period, the value of banks' assets continuously increases, and this leads to additional credit provisions. In such circumstances, banks look for new investing projects that favor booming markets. When the economy slows down, the market collapses since the prices are based on excessive and overenthusiastic credit provision of banks. The large write-downs and decreased asset prices also affect earnings.

The use of Fair Values in financial reporting enhances the predictive ability of earnings only during periods of relatively lower credit risk. During years in which credit risk is high, we don't believe that any association between increased use of FVA in financial reporting and the ability of earnings to predict future cash flows exists. During financial crises and periods of economic distress, assets' prices may reflect the amount of liquidity available in the market rather than the future earnings power of the assets (Allen & Carletti, 2008). Economic cyclical fluctuations, as the basic economic operations in the macroeconomy, can exert a direct influence on earnings persistence by affecting firm fundamentals as well as EM. The macroeconomic environment can affect firm fundamentals, which in turn affects earnings persistence. In general, during turbulent financial periods EQ decreases since earnings manipulation increases. Earnings are more persistent when growth rates are high (i.e., in an expansion) and production is high (e.g., in a credit crunch period) than when the growth rates are low (i.e., in a recession) and the production is low, respectively. Hence, earnings persistence declines consistently when going from an expansion to a moderate growth phase and then to a recession. Therefore, earnings persistence significantly declines when the economic climate worsens.

Previous studies provided empirical evidence of the effects of the 2008 financial crisis on financial reporting and earnings manipulation (e.g., Arthur, Tang, & Lin, 2015; De Luca & Paolone, 2019; Dimitras, Kyriakou, & Iatridis, 2015; Filip & Raffournier, 2014; Habib, Bhuiyan, & Islam, 2013; Iatridis & Dimitras, 2013; Kousenidis, Ladas, & Negakis, 2013; Persakis & Iatridis, 2016). During a financial crisis, firms face increased difficulties, lower and more volatile earnings, poor performance, financial critical issues, and also a lack of investors' confidence. However, the financial crisis may also have a positive effect by encouraging managers to improve the transparency of financial reporting in order to increase investors' confidence and to attract potential investors. According to prior literature concerning the impact of the 2008 financial crisis[7] on EQ in the EU context, it is noted that financial crisis had a significant impact on firms' financial reporting. A period of economic recession is usually characterized as to be a period of economic turbulence, where market uncertainty is greater than in normal economic periods. Moreover, in these circumstances investors' confidence decreases, and firms experience a poor performance and several financial distresses. Moreover, earnings tend to be more volatile, to show a decreasing pattern and to incorporate more losses (Kousenidis et al., 2013). Nevertheless, the effect of the financial crisis on EQ is unclear. Some studies argue that in such periods, firms have more incentives to increase the quality of financial reporting, e.g., to enhance investors' confidence. EQ can be higher during a financial crisis period if it motivates managers to enhance EQ in an attempt to boost investor assurance and to reduce the negative impact of the economic downturn (Arthur et al., 2015).

The results indicate a higher quality of earnings during the crisis period because firms that face liquidity problems and depend on external financing have strong incentives to improve earnings in order to attract potential investors. To sum it up, financial crisis is an uncommon circumstance during which firms achieve poor performance, have low and volatile earnings, and face financial needs of liquidity which is limited in these periods

[7] The financial crisis began in 2007 in the USA, but only in 2008 reached its peak with the failure of several financial institutions (Lehman Brothers, Merrill Lynch, Fannie Mae, Freddie Mac, Washington Mutual, Wachovia, Citigroup, and AIG). However, the consequences of the crisis began to be felt in Europe mainly in 2008 (Filip & Raffournier, 2014). As such, the period 2006–2007 is considered pre-crisis period, 2008–2012 the crisis period, and 2013–2016 the post-crisis period.

due to lack of investors' confidence (Arthur et al., 2015). This might encourage firms to engage in less EM and then to increase EQ as a signal to attract potential investors and to obtain external financing (Kousenidis et al., 2013). In periods of financial turmoil when there is greater market volatility, high-quality earnings allow users of financial statements to make less risky and more efficient decisions.

Another reason is the increasing monitoring by creditors, auditors, and other stakeholders during the crisis which pressure managers to reduce the degree of EM (Chia, Lapsley, & Lee, 2007). Moreover, as during a crisis poor performance is already expected, the market is more predisposed to tolerate this worse performance, and hence firm's incentives to manage earnings reduce (Arthur et al., 2015; Filip & Raffournier, 2014). Lastly, if managers are concerned with investor confidence, they will have incentives to provide more credible and transparent financial reports, thus reducing information asymmetry and improving investor confidence (Arthur et al., 2015).

On the other hand, it is argued that managers can be led to manipulate earnings during this period in an attempt to mask the negative effects of the crisis, perhaps because of companies' bad financial performance and low earnings (Arthur et al., 2015; Filip & Raffournier, 2014). In fact, some studies, such as those of Iatridis and Dimitras (2013), found a decrease in the quality of financial reporting during periods of economic recession as managers engage more in EM to improve low profitability and to accommodate their higher debt. Other empirical results (Persakis & Iatridis, 2016) also indicated a decrease in EQ during the financial crisis, especially in the countries with weaker shareholders' protection. The increase of EM suggests that managers opportunistically smooth income to beat earnings' targets (Rusmin, Scully, & Tower, 2013).

5.5.1 *Fair Value Accounting and Earnings Management*

In the last decade, there is an extensive attention from researchers to investigate the determinants and the consequences of EM. They claimed that managers' incentives to manipulate earnings are mostly influenced by a poor cash flow position; obsolete inventory, receivables that are not collectible; unrealistic revenue and profit outlooks; analyst's expectations; and violated restrictive loan covenants. Except for firms' attributes which can cause earnings manipulation, there are particular events creating incentives to manage earnings (Strobl, 2013). For example, managers of financially distressed firms tend to engage more in income-decreasing practices compared to their healthy firm counterparts (Habib et al., 2013). Moreover, there are a number of situations in which EM is used: (1) transferring earnings from "good" years to "bad" years, (2) postponing income recognition to reduce tax burden, (3) the willingness of companies to reveal positive results correlated with the trend of postponing negative results, and (4) options of managers to use discretionary accounting policies in order to increase their current or future compensation (entitled to stock options or bonus schemes).

However, also a financial crisis influences the managers' incentives to produce financial reports that may show an overly positive picture of a firm's business activities and financial position. There is some evidence about the impacts of bad economic conditions (e.g., the existence of bankruptcy or delisting) on EM and on the quality of earnings (e.g., Cimini, 2014; Filip & Raffournier, 2014; Habib et al., 2013; Iatridis and Dimitras, 2013; Kousenidis et al., 2013). In accounting and finance literature, several papers have investigated the managers' incentives for earnings manipulation in these circumstances. Particularly, some authors examined the firm's financial motives for EM, and they concluded that firms wanting to meet and/or exceed financial analysts' earnings forecasts (e.g., firms with low profitability and high leverage measures) are likely to use EM. Listed companies tend to engage more in EM to improve their lower profitability and liquidity during a financial crisis. Kousenidis et al. (2013) inspected whether and to what extent the 2008 financial crisis in the European Union had effects on EM and on the quality of the reported earnings of listed firms. The results show that on average EQ has improved during the financial crisis and EM is sensitive to the business cycle. The economic cyclical fluctuations can exercise a direct influence on the earnings persistence of a company by affecting firm fundamentals as well as EM. EM is used either in good economic conditions or in bad economic conditions, and the choice of manipulating earnings is focused on investor's perspectives. During prosperous periods, firms have incentives to manage earnings downwards, while in recession period the overall performance of a firm declines and managers usually have incentives to manage earnings upwards to hide them in order to protect the future needs.

In this respect, macroeconomic conditions have the potential to influence EM, but the relationship seems to be inverse. Managers should have less motivation to manipulate earnings in recession periods due to a higher market tolerance for poor performance. On the contrary, managers are expected to engage in opportunistic behaviors in economic booms. During a financial crisis or a financial downturn, investors' pessimism is dominant and any good news is overlapped from bad news (e.g., when the dissolutions of business increase dramatically). As most of the investors react to bad news by further reducing the firms' access to capital, managers have an incentive to recognize more positive news than they normally do. In an attempt to cope with these negative reactions, managers choose more aggressive conservatism during the financial crisis. In this regard, we believe that financial crisis is one factor that influences the extent of conservatism practiced by managers[8] as conservatism is significantly higher during economic contractions (Jenkins, Kane, & Velury, 2009). Higher conservative earnings result in a lower degree of EM in recession periods. Particularly, managers have an incentive to choose more aggressive conservatism, to lower earnings predictability, and to book more accruals. Hence, we assume that firms characterized by more conservative accounting significantly experience less value losses during a crisis period compared to their less conservative counterparts.

A systematic crisis causes more companies to fall into a financial distress, and in this situation, companies would be exposed to higher information asymmetries and more agency problems. Agency problems become more severe during the crisis period because the expected return on investment falls. In this circumstance, unlike the previously mentioned scenario, managers can be more likely to involve in aggressive earnings manipulations using private information for their private benefits. In this situation, managers are more likely to manipulate accounting numbers opportunistically using private information for their private benefits (engage in aggressive EM). Thus, greater earnings' manipulation involves increased risk on shareholders and could lead to more negative returns and subsequent firm value losses. When the economy is flourishing, investors may pay less attention to the quality of earnings because investment opportunities are abundant.

[8] Cfr. LaFond and Watts (2008) contend that "conservative financial reporting is a governance mechanism that reduces the managers' ability to manipulate and overstate financial performance and increases the firm's cash flows and value".

During a crisis, greater earnings' manipulations impose amplified information and agency risks on investors resulting in more negative returns. In this regard, conservatism[9]—as an efficient disciplining mechanism—lessens agency and information risks, thereby moderating losses of firm value during crisis periods. The intrinsic asymmetric verification requirements of conservative accounting limit managerial earnings' manipulations, thereby providing more reliable and transparent accounting information to external investors (Watts, 2003a). If conservatism plays an important role in mitigating information asymmetries and agency problems between managers and external shareholders, we suppose that conservative accounting impacts on shareholders' value significantly during the crisis period.

Nevertheless, opponents of conservatism argue that it introduces biases into financial reporting because it amplifies information asymmetry and leads users of financial reports—including investors—to make inappropriate suggestions probably. Consequently, conservatism could potentially cause inefficient resource allocations and the reduction of firm value.[10]

5.5.2 *Fair Value Accounting and Earnings Management in Banking Sector*

Banks and other financial institutions are especially subject to FVA, since assets and liabilities most affected by FVA—i.e., financial instruments—represent a significant share of their balance sheets. As a consequence, FVA has been blamed especially for increased volatility of earnings. Therefore, the debate on the appropriateness and the effects of FVA has been animated especially within the banking sector. Proponents of FVA have suggested several benefits. First, FVA better reflects the bank's exposure toward risks, especially during volatile periods, by capturing risks not

[9] Watts (2003a, 2003b) argues that conservatism is an important feature of financial reporting in ensuring efficient contracting between shareholders and debt holders and between shareholders and managers by limiting managerial bias and the risk of opportunistic payments (e.g., compensation, dividends).

[10] The Financial Accounting Standard Board (FASB) holds a similar perspective. In 2010, the FASB removed conservatism from its conceptual framework, and it argues that conservatism could produce information asymmetries and that "describing prudence or conservatism as a qualitative characteristic or a desirable response to uncertainty would conflict with the quality of neutrality" (FASB, Conceptual Framework for Financial Reporting. Statement of Financial Accounting Concepts No. 8, September 2010).

detained by non-Fair Value measures of income (Hodder et al., 2006). Thus, FVA enhances efficiency of market discipline and leads to a prompt detection of insolvent banks. Second, income smoothing and EM are conceivable under HCA (if corporate results worsen, management can influence reported income by selling revalued assets) where under FVA the possibility of income smoothing is reduced: The asset is recognized at Fair Value, and the gain/loss from its revaluation is reflected in the income statement when it is generated.

On the contrary, opponents of FVA claim that it increases the volatility of bank's earnings and it reduces their predictability. Second, the transparency in valuation and performance measurement may be dubious in illiquid markets or when several valuation techniques (based on unobservable inputs) are used in a single financial report. Third, the use of FVA may lead to excessive leverage in booms and write-downs in busts, thus causing pro-cyclicality (Laux & Leuz, 2009, 2010).[11]

The literature on EM by banks is quite extensive. Goel and Thakor (2003) distinguished between real and artificial EM. The latter is attained through the reporting of flexibility provided by some accounting principles, and it has a negative effect on firm value since it undermines the credibility of financial statements and misleads investors and other stakeholders. Several motivations have been suggested for banks' managers to affect or misrepresent earnings data by using this type of EM, allowed by—or a consequence of—Accounting Standards. First, explicit management of earnings may be a way for banks to signal a good quality of their business and balance sheets. Second, accounting rules allow for discretion in certain items, such as loss provisions, which affect the book value of capital. Hence, EM could result from accounting practices intended to meet minimum capital requirements set by the monetary authority. Third, an inter-temporal averaging of reported economic earnings could make net income looks less volatile. In the banking industry, managers

[11] More comprehensive accounts of the pros and cons of FVA and further references can be found in Landsman (2007), Penman (2007), Benston (2008), Laux and Leuz (2009).

would have incentives for income smoothing in order to signal low exposure to risk or to attain stable compensation objectives (Dechow, Ge, & Schrand, 2010; Healy & Wahlen, 1999).[12]

The typical instrument associated with EM is the use of discretionary accruals (accrual-based EM). In the banking sector, analyses have focused on the manipulation of reserves and, more specifically, of the loan loss provision (LLP). Bank managers can use the LLP to reduce the volatility of the reported earnings—earnings smoothing—or to influence regulatory capital measures (Tier 1) to avoid violating regulatory capital requirements, among other objectives (Curcio & Hasan, 2014). Regarding the bank capital adequacy, strong capital buffers ensure a sufficient bank capital to absorb unexpected losses and external shocks. Hence, banks use LLP as a form of capital which can be increased (decreased) when capital is low (high). The basic strategy to smooth earnings is to understate (overstate) the provisions when earnings are low (high) in order to mitigate the adverse (positive) effects of other factors on earnings. Fair Value measurement relies on managerial assumptions, and in this regard, supporters argue that giving managers more discretion in Fair Value measurement conveys more relevant information. On the contrary, critics argue that greater flexibility in Fair Value measurements could be opportunistically exploited by managers and adversely affect the reliability of financial reporting. From this point of view, the unreliability of mark to market valuations originates from manager's desire to manipulate earnings.

In this regard, some analysts point out the danger of an excessive decision-making power of the banks regarding the determination of provisions—given that this would allow them to use the provisions to level profits—reducing the transparency of the financial statements and consequently their usefulness for investors and counterparties. To avoid this situation, the provisioning criteria must be clear on the conditions and methods of setting up provisions and adjusting them over time, as well as on transparency relating to methodologies and assumptions (Cohen & Edwards, 2017). By the way, IFRS 9 poses some interesting challenges regarding the impairment model of financial instruments. Decisions around classification of financial assets into different stages (three bucket model) and the calculation of the expected credit losses (ECL)

[12] A reduction of taxes paid has also been suggested as a motivation for EM, but empirical evidence in this regard has been scarce (Beatty, Chamberlain, & Magliolo, 1995; Collins, Shackelford, & Wahlen, 1995).

require the consideration of forward-looking information to faithfully reflect the deterioration of credit risk since initial recognition. The IFRS 9 impairment model results in an earlier recognition of credit losses following an expected loss model (versus the previous incurred loss model of IAS 39) for provisions.

While prior research documents the existence of potential manipulation of Fair Value estimates (Dechow et al., 2010; Ozili, 2015; Vyas, 2010), there is relatively little empirical evidence specifically inspecting whether additional managerial discretion (allowed by Accounting Standards for Fair Value measurement) reveals more about a firm's economic fundamentals or degrades the quality of earnings.[13]

We extend the emerging literature on managerial discretion in Fair Value estimates to investigate the following questions: "What are the effects of additional discretion in FVA allowed by Accounting Standards on bank's earnings?" and "What is the relation between the application of FVA in practice and the quality of bank's earnings?"

In examining the quality of earnings, the focus is on two attributes: reliability and relevance. These are two qualities of financial information used by both the FASB and the IASB in Standard setting. Both the FASB and the IASB allow banks more flexibility in applying their Fair Value Accounting providing an opportunity to examine the effects of increased managerial discretion in Fair Value measurement on banks' EQ.

Although the use of FVA looks credibly rational in well operating markets, the reliability, relevance, and integrity of this approach decrease when markets do not run. In these circumstances, Fair Values are likely to be measured through valuation techniques which allow EM and could result in lower quality of reported earnings. Valuation of Fair Value (mark to model) opens doors for the application of management judgment and intended prejudice which can reduce the quality of financial reporting (Paoloni, Paolucci, & Menicucci, 2017).

As part of a research project carried out in the banking sector, we have investigated the influence of FVA on EQ in European banks over the 2007–2016 period as financial reporting system of banks is particularly exposed to FVA. Findings have shown that under an FVA-based

[13]See the debate between Dechow et al. (2010) and Barth and Taylor (2010) on whether Fair Value estimates of securitization gains are manipulated by managers. Barth and Taylor (2010) show that the evidence of this issue is inconclusive and further investigation is needed.

accounting system, earnings have high-quality ranks for banks in European countries. Specifically, we have discovered primary evidence that Fair Value gains (losses) recognized through profit or loss (FVTPL) and through other comprehensive income (FVTOCI) are positively associated with banks' EQ.

We have examined an unbalanced panel dataset of 5030 commercial European banks, generating 50,300 observations over a 10-year period from 2007 to 2016. Within the sample selection, we have analyzed any active bank operating in Europe and having complete, consistent, and accessible dataset for each of the years of the time period chosen for the analysis. We have computed an aggregate EQ measure (AEQ) based on four single EQ measures: persistence, predictability, variability, and smoothness.[14]

In line with the research specified hypothesis regarding the association between IAS/IFRSs' adoption and EQ, the findings confirmed that the application of FVA increases AEQ. The movement from HCA toward FVA is appraised to result in more relevant, timely, credible, and transparent financial statements. The application of Fair Value enhances the relevance of the reported numbers because it reflects market values and it has more economical meaning than HCA. Within the implemented regression model overall statistically significant (R-square of 0.572016), the coefficient of relative amount of FVTPL resulted positive and statistically significant (coefficient = 87.30902, p-value = 0.0082), suggesting that European banks with more income components recognized at FVTPL have a higher AEQ. Similar results can be found for Fair Value gains (losses) reported through FVTOCI. Estimated coefficient of the amount of FVTOCI has also been positive and statistically significant (coefficient = 241.9954, p-value = 0.0036), revealing that European banks with large percentage of income components recognized at FVTOCI have a higher AEQ.

5.6 Conclusions

Regarding the relationship between the application of FVA and EQ, there is mixed evidence and the majority of prior studies on this topic is mainly performed in common law countries such as the USA, the UK,

[14] For a closer discussion, see Chapter 2.

or Australia. The shift from HCA toward FVA in European legislation after the implementation of IAS/IFRSs originated by the assumed belief of high quality and decision relevance of market-based measures than those of cost-based ones. In this regard, managerial assumptions for Fair Value measurement delivers more relevant information, but greater discretionary could undesirably affect the reliability of financial reporting, especially when this discretionary is opportunistically used by managers.

The following conclusions on FVA and EQ can be derived. The use of Fair Value may impact differently on EQ due to several reasons. FVA involves more current accounting information for investors since it is a market-based measurement.

In this regard, FVA is a relevant accounting criterion although we cannot support this assumption in all circumstances as in illiquid markets companies use valuation techniques to estimate Fair Value. Specifically, in the case of illiquid or inactive markets, prices are not directly observable (mark to market) and valuation inputs are not easily available. Consequently, the adopted estimates are possibly based on discretionary parameters. Moreover, in these situations prices are not able to reflect the Fair Value that should be evaluated assuming internal estimation models (mark to model). When managers don't have observable and objectively measurable inputs to assess Fair Values in valuation process, the reliability of Fair Value estimates can be potentially affected by errors due to specific hypothesis and parameters adopted by managers. Hence, Fair Value is considered unreliable in inefficient markets because it is particularly subject to managerial discretion in this case. High amount of subjective judgments and intentional bias in Fair Value estimation can reduce the quality of financial reporting since management opportunities for the exercise of discretion can result in a higher opportunistic EM and thus in a reduced amount of EQ.

Certain decisions made by management have an impact on the quality of earnings because they can expand or damage it. On one hand, discretionary accounting choices can be regarded as an efficient communication of private information and expectations that improve the informativeness of a firm's current and future performance. On the other hand, the devious manipulation of earnings by managers may mislead the usefulness of financial reporting to stakeholders. An increase in managerial discretion in Fair Value measurement is associated with a higher probability of EM and lower earnings informativeness (Fargher & Zhang, 2014). In this case, EM looks like a practice that could lower the quality of earnings if it identifies with the result of opportunistic use of accruals and earnings smoothing with the intent to misinform users. Managers can use both their privileged knowledge about the firm in preparing financial reporting and their discretion in manipulating earnings to the detriment of the external users' interests (i.e., information asymmetry and conflict of interests between insiders and stakeholders). Managers can also have several incentives to manipulate earnings both for their own benefits (e.g., earnings-based compensation and bonus compensation) and to meet analysts' expectations or to influence the stock price.

Even without the managers' intended distortion of financial reporting, the more subjective nature of Level 3 Fair Value estimates within the Fair Value hierarchy valuation potentially leads to greater information asymmetry and therefore to greater estimation error. The reliability of FVA depends on the application of the Fair Value hierarchy, and especially it is influenced by the degree of transparency in the valuation process and the discretionary use of unobservable inputs and biased estimates that could identify opportunistic management behaviors. As a consequence, the reliability of Fair Value is related to management manipulations within the estimation process, and the correlation between FVA and EQ depends on the discretion exercised by managers within the limits allowed by the Accounting Standards. From this point of view and considering the mentioned aspects all together, we conclude that higher exposure to FVA is negatively related to EQ if it favors EM practices that compromise the quality of the earnings in terms of reliability. This is because FVA grants management involvement in the estimation of Level 3 inputs when market values are not directly observable.

The impact of FVA on EQ does not involve the conceptual validity of this accounting criterion but has to be extended to its practical application in some market conditions. When FVA relies on management accounting discretion, this potentially undermines estimates within the Fair Value hierarchy and then the quality of financial reporting. On the contrary, in efficient and liquid markets, Fair Value-based information is highly relevant from an investor's perspective because Fair Values reflect market prices. In such scenario, we cannot consider IAS/IFRSs as a barrier for EQ, and in particular, Fair Value provides reliable and accurate financial information which supports the decision-making process. It is accepted that sometimes FVA does not add to the comprehension of enterprise value, but we admit that it has enough advantages in order to present qualitative and reliable information in efficient-market hypothesis (EMH).

Bibliography

Allen, F., & Carletti, E. (2008). Mark-to-market accounting and liquidity pricing. *Journal of Accounting and Economics, 45*(2), 358–378.

Arthur, N., Tang, Q., & Lin, Z. (2015). Corporate accruals quality during the 2008–2010 global financial crisis. *Journal of International Accounting, Auditing and Taxation, 25,* 1–15.

Barth, M. E. (2004). Fair values and financial statement volatility in the market discipline across countries and industries. In C. Borio, W. C. Hunter, G. G. Kaufman, & K. Tsatsaronis (Eds.), *Market discipline across countries and industries.* Cambridge, MA: MIT Press.

Barth, M. E. (2008). Global financial reporting: Implications for U.S. academics. *The Accounting Review, 83*(5), 1159–1179.

Barth, M. E., & Landsman, W. R. (2010). How did financial reporting contribute to the financial crisis? *European Accounting Review, 19*(1), 399–423.

Barth, M. E., & Taylor, D. J. (2010). In defence of fair value: Weighing the evidence on earnings management and asset securitizations. *Journal of Accounting and Economics, 49*(1–2), 26–33.

Beatty, A., Chamberlain, S. L., & Magliolo, J. (1995). Managing financial reports of commercial banks: The influence of taxes, regulatory capital, and earnings. *Journal of Accounting Research, 33*(2), 231–261.

Benston, G. J. (2008). The shortcomings of fair-value accounting described in SFAS 157. *Journal of Accounting and Public Policy, 27*(2), 101–114.

Bhat, B., Frankel, R., & Martin, X. (2011). Panacea, Pandora's box, or placebo: Feedback in bank mortgage-backed security holdings and fair value accounting. *Journal of Accounting and Economics, 52,* 153–173.

Bonaci, C., Matis, D., & Strouhal, J. (2010). Crisis of fair value measurement? Some defence of the best of all bad measurement bases. *WSEAS Transactions on Business and Economics, 7*(2), 114–125.

Bowen, R. M., Khan, U., & Rajgopal, S. (2009). *The economic consequences of relaxing fair value accounting and impairment rules on banks during the financial crisis of 2008–2009* (Working Paper), University of Washington.

Callao Gastón, S., & Jarne, J. I. (2010). Have IFRS affected earnings management in the European Union? *Accounting in Europe, 7*(2), 159–189.

Chia, Y., Lapsley, I., & Lee, H. W. (2007). Choice of auditors and earnings management during the Asian financial crisis. *Managerial Auditing Journal, 22,* 177–196.

Chisnall, P. (2001). Fair value accounting—An industry view. *Balance Sheet, 9*(1), 27–33.

Cimini, R. (2014). How has the financial crisis affected earnings management? A European study. *Applied Economics, 47*(3), 302–317.

Cohen, B. H., Edwards, G. A., Jr. (2017). La nuova era degli accantonamenti per perdite attese su crediti. *Rassegna trimestrale BRI*, marzo, 1–20.

Collins, J. H., Shackelford, D. A., & Wahlen, J. M. (1995). Bank differences in the coordination of regulatory capital, earnings and taxes. *Journal of Accounting Research, 33*(2), 263–291.

Curcio, D., & Hasan, I. (2014). Earnings and capital management and signaling: The use of loan-loss provisions by European banks. *The European Journal of Finance, 21*(1), 26–50.

Dechow, P. M., Ge, W., & Schrand, C. (2010). Understanding earnings quality: A review of the proxies, their determinants and their consequences. *Journal of Accounting and Economics, 50*(2–3), 344–401.

De Luca, F., & Paolone, F. (2019). The impact of the financial crisis on earnings management: Empirical evidence from Italian and Spanish listed companies. *Corporate Ownership & Control, 16*(2), 121–130.

Dimitras, A. I., Kyriakou, M. I., & Iatridis, G. (2015). Financial crisis, GDP variation and earnings management in Europe. *Research in International Business and Finance, 34,* 338–354.

Dimitropoulos, P. E., Asteriou, D., Kousenidis, D., & Leventis, S. (2013). The impact of IFRS on accounting quality: Evidence from Greece. *Advances in Accounting, 29*(1), 108–123.

Donnelly, R. (2002). Earnings persistence, losses and the estimation of earnings response coefficients. *Abacus, 38*(1), 121–133.

Fargher, N., & Zhang, J. (2014). Changes in the measurement of fair value: Implications for accounting earnings. *Accounting Forum, 38*(3), 184–199.

Filip, A., & Raffournier, B. (2014). Financial crisis and earnings management: The European evidence. *International Journal of Accounting, 49*(4), 455–478.

Goel, A., & Thakor, A. V. (2003). Why do firms smooth earnings? *The Journal of Business, 76*(1), 151–192.

Habib, A., Bhuiyan, M. B. U., & Islam, A. (2013). Financial distress, earnings management and market pricing of accruals during the global financial crisis. *Managerial Finance, 39*(2), 155–180.

Hasanzade, M., Darabi, R., & Mahfoozi, G. (2013). Factors affecting the earnings response coefficient: An empirical study for Iran. *European Online Journal of Natural and Social Sciences, 2*(3), 2551–2560.

Healy, P. M., & Wahlen, J. M. (1999). A review of the earnings management literature and its implications for standard setting. *Accounting Horizons, 13*(4), 365–383.

Hitz, J. M. (2007). The decision usefulness of fair value accounting—A theoretical perspective. *European Accounting Review, 16*(2), 323–362.

Hodder, L. D., Hopkins, P. E., & Wahlen, J. M. (2006). Risk-relevance of fair-value income measures for commercial banks. *The Accounting Review, 81*(2), 337–375.

Hung, M. (2000). Accounting standards and value relevance of financial statements: An international analysis. *Journal of Accounting and Economics, 30*(3), 401–420.

Iatridis, G., & Dimitras, A. I. (2013). Financial crisis and accounting quality: Evidence from five European countries. *Advances in Accounting, 29*(1), 154–160.

Jenkins, D., Kane, G. D., & Velury, U. (2009). Earnings conservatism and value relevance across the business cycle. *Journal of Business Finance & Accounting, 36*(9–10), 1041–1058.

Khan, U. (2011). *Does fair value accounting contribute to systemic risk in the banking industry?* Columbia Business School Research Paper.

King, A. M. (2008). Be careful what you ask for: Is fair value accounting really fair? *International Journal of Disclosure and Governance, 5*(4), 301–311.

Kousenidis, D. V., Ladas, A. C., & Negakis, P. (2013). The effects of the European debt crisis on earnings quality. *International Review of Financial Analysis, 30,* 351–362.

LaFond, R., & Watts, R. L. (2008). The information role of conservatism. *The Accounting Review, 83*(2), 447–478.

Landsman, W. R. (2007). Is fair value accounting information relevant and reliable? Evidence from capital market research. *Accounting and Business Research, 37*(s-1), 19–30.

Laux, C., & Leuz, C. (2009). The crisis of fair-value accounting: Making sense of the recent debate. *Accounting, Organizations and Society, 34*(6–7), 826–834.

Laux, C., & Leuz, C. (2010). Did fair value accounting contribute to the financial crisis? *Journal of Economic Perspectives, 24*(1), 93–118.

Lo, K. (2008). Earnings management and earnings quality. *Journal of Accounting and Economics, 45*(2–3), 350–357.

Lobo, G. J., & Zhou, J. (2001). Disclosure quality and earnings management. *Asian-Pacific Journal of Accounting and Economics, 8*(1), 1–20.

Magnan, M. L. (2009). Fair value accounting and the financial crisis: Messenger or contributor? *Accounting Perspectives, 8*(3), 189–213.

Menicucci, E. (2015). *Fair value accounting: Key issues arising from the financial crisis.* Basingstoke, UK: Palgrave Macmillan.

Menicucci, E., & Paolucci, G. (2016). Fair value accounting and financial crisis: A literature-based analysis. *Journal of Financial Reporting & Accounting, 14*(1), 49–71.

Nissim, D. (2003). Reliability of banks' fair value disclosure for loans. *Review of Quantitative Finance and Accounting, 20*(4), 355–384.

Ozili, P. K. (2015). Loan loss provisioning, income smoothing, signaling, capital management and procyclicality: Does IFRS matter? Empirical evidence from Nigeria. *Mediterranean Journal of Social Sciences, 6*(2), 224–232.

Paoloni, M., Paolucci, G., & Menicucci, E. (2017). Fair value accounting and earnings quality (EQ) in banking sector: Evidence from Europe. *African Journal of Business Management, 11*(20), 597–607.

Penman, S. (2007). Financial reporting quality: Is fair value a plus or a minus? *Accounting and Business Research, 37*(s-1), 33–44.

Persakis, A., & Iatridis, G. E. (2016). Audit quality, investor protection and earnings management during the financial crisis of 2008: An international perspective. *Journal of International Financial Markets, Institutions and Money, 41,* 73–101.

Plantin, G., Sapra, H., & Shin, H. S. (2008). Marking-to-market: Panacea or Pandora's box? *Journal of Accounting Research, 46*(2), 435–460.

Pompili, M., & Tutino, M. (2019a). Fair value accounting and management opportunism on earnings management in banking sector: First evidence: The impact of unobservable inputs on earning quality. *Corporate Ownership & Control, 15*(2), 59–69.

Pompili, M., & Tutino, M. (2019b). Fair value accounting and earning management: The impact of unobservable inputs on earning quality. *Corporate Ownership & Control, 16*(2), 8–18.

Ronen, J., & Yaari, V. (2008). *Earnings management: Emerging insights in theory, practice and research.* New York: Springer.

Rusmin, R., Scully, G., & Tower, G. (2013). Income smoothing behavior by Asian transportation firms. *Managerial Auditing Journal, 28*(1), 23–44.

Siekkinen, J. (2016). Value relevance of fair values in different investor protection environments. *Accounting Forum, 40*(1), 1–15.

Sŏdan, S. (2015). The impact of fair value accounting on earnings quality in eastern European countries. *Procedia Economics and Finance, 32,* 1769–1786.

Song, C., Thomas, W., & Yi, H. (2010). Value relevance of FAS No. 157 fair value hierarchy information and the impact of corporate governance mechanisms. *Accounting Review, 85*(4), 1375–1410.

Strobl, G. (2013). Earnings manipulation and the cost of capital. *Journal of Accounting Research, 51*(2), 449–473.

Sun, J., Cahan, S. F., & Emanuel, D. (2011). How would the mandatory adoption of IFRS affect the earnings quality of U.S. firms? Evidence from cross-listed firms in the U.S. *Accounting Horizons, 25*(4), 837–860.

Tutino, M., & Pompili, M. (2019). Fair value accounting and management opportunism on earnings management in banking sector. *Corporate Ownership and Control, 15*(2), 1–12.

Veron, N. (2008). Fair value accounting is the wrong scapegoat for the crisis. *Accounting in Europe, 44*(2), 63–69.

Vyas, D. (2010). The timeliness of accounting write-downs by U.S. financial institutions during the financial crisis of 2007–2008. *Journal of Accounting Research, 49*(3), 823–860.

Watts, R. (2003a). Conservatism in accounting, part I: Explanations and implications. *Accounting Horizons, 17*(3), 207–221.

Watts, R. (2003b). Conservatism in accounting, part II: Evidence and research opportunities. *Accounting Horizons, 17*(4), 287–301.

Whittington, G. (2008). Fair value and the IASB/FASB conceptual framework project: An alternative view. *Abacus, 44*(2), 139–168.

Index

E. Menicucci, *Earnings Quality*,
https://doi.org/10.1007/978-3-030-36798-5

T

U

V

W

The manufacturer's authorised representative in the EU is Springer Nature Customer Service Centre GmbH, Europaplatz 3, 69115 Heidelberg, Germany. If you have any concerns regarding our products, please contact ProductSafety@springernature.com

Printed and bound by CPI Group (UK) Ltd, Croydon, CR0 4YY

30/09/2026

02225609-0009